THE RED AND
THE BLACK

NOTES

including

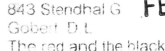

by
D. L. Gobert, Ph.D.
Department of Forei
Southern Illinois Uni

LINC

Editor

Gary Carey, M.A.
University of Colorado

Consulting Editor

James L. Roberts, Ph.D.
Department of English
University of Nebraska

ISBN 0-8220-1111-5

Cliffs Notes, Inc.   Lincoln, Nebraska

CONTENTS

The Red and the Black

STENDHAL'S LIFE AND WORK

Henri Beyle (Stendhal) was born in 1783, in Grenoble, into a respectable, middle-class family. Chérubin Beyle, Stendhal's father, a reactionary in politics, was an industrious, narrow-minded bourgeois, whom Henri detested and to whom he later referred as the "bâtard." Stendhal loved his mother tenderly, but this delightful woman, whose origin Stendhal liked to think was Italian, died when he was only seven. Later, he idealized her memory just as he exaggerated the mediocrity of his father. Of a fiery and rebellious nature, Stendhal declared himself early to be an atheist and "jacobin," or liberal—an expression of revolt, no doubt, against his father.

Stendhal studied at the Ecole Centrale in Grenoble until 1799, excelling in mathematics and art. Thirsting for adventure, he went to Paris, and securing a commission in the army, sojourned briefly in Italy, a country he came to love above France. Back in Paris, Stendhal resigned from the army, and from 1802 until 1806, he studied the eighteenth-century materialistic philosophers, Helvétius and Cabanis, and aspired unsuccessfully to become a playwright. A highly placed relative obtained for Stendhal an administrative position in the army that took him to Germany, with periodic trips back to Paris. In 1812, he participated in Napoleon's Russian retreat.

Stendhal's first literary endeavors were biographies, *Vies de Haydn, de Mozart, et de Métastase,* written in 1815 in Milan, where he lived as a dilettante, fraternizing with Italian liberals, delighting in Italian art and music. He was so taken with Italy, and in particular with Milan, that he requested that his epitaph read: "Henri Beyle, Milanais." He believed that Italy afforded a more propitious atmosphere for the pursuit of the cult of energy than did more prosaic, post-Napoleonic France. Turning to art criticism, he wrote *Histoire de la Peinture en Italie* (1817), and addressing himself to tourism, *Rome, Naples, et Florence* (1817).

Stendhal's unsuccessful love affair with Méthilde Dembowski inspired him to write the autobiographical treatise, *De l'Amour* (1822). Méthilde served as a model for various of Stendhal's subsequent heroines. The treatise analyzes the mechanism of love as Stendhal had observed it operating in himself. The second part of the work is a pseudo-sociological study purporting to show how national temperament influences and modifies the love mechanism. Stendhal was forced to leave Milan in 1821 because of his liberal political beliefs.

Back in Paris from 1821 until 1830, Stendhal experienced financial hardships. In 1823 and 1825, he published parts I and II, respectively, of *Racine et Shakespeare*, in which he praised Shakespeare as superior in psychological analysis to the classical Racine. The work elaborates the prevailing romantic view in esthetics that proclaimed the relativism of beauty. Stendhal saw in Romanticism the latest manifestation of the beautiful. In Part II of the work, Stendhal addressed himself to the comic, attempted to define it, and proclaimed Molière, the French classical comic genius, to be a literary anachronism. Stendhal seemed to favor Shakespeare only when the latter italianized his plays. Stendhal's cult of energy caused him to execrate contemplatives such as Hamlet.

At the age of forty-four, Stendhal wrote his first novel, *Armance*, which neither his friends nor the public acclaimed. It was intended as a psychological study of Octave, an impotent who ultimately commits suicide. Octave's physical anomaly prefigures and is symbolic of the Stendhalian hero's inability to accept life as offered by Restoration society. The Stendhalian theme of the pursuit of individual happiness is already apparent, but Octave is unsuccessful in his search, preferring suicide to compromise as a solution to his dilemma. Stendhal's own reserve and the prevailing mores prevented him from clarifying the nature of Octave's affliction for the reader, and the resulting ambiguity was the reason that the public found the hero enigmatic. The society that Octave opposes with such violence is not minutely described by the novelist, therefore the social dimension of the novel is unconvincing.

Turning away from the novel, Stendhal composed *Promenades dans Rome* (1829), utilizing surplus material from his earlier travelogs and notes offered by a cousin. The work has been called a glorified guidebook, by which is meant that Stendhal's original perceptions and impressions illuminate many pages of what would otherwise simply be a book of tourism. In this work Stendhal again exposed the concept of relativism in esthetics, proclaiming that the concept of the beautiful varies from age to age and among cultures.

The realistic note that runs through Stendhal's literary endeavors — fictional, biographical, documentary, critical, and journalistic — stems from his need to anchor himself solidly in reality as a point of departure. Everything he wrote begins in the realm of facts. He imposes his impressions and transforms reality, but it is a reality exterior to himself that furnishes the plot or subject matter.

Thus, *The Red and the Black, Chronicle of the XIX Century*, written in 1829 and published in 1831, fictionalizes and elaborates an actual happening of which Stendhal had read in records of court proceedings.

The historical person who served as a model for Julien Sorel was a certain Antoine Berthet, convicted, like Julien, of murder in December, 1827, at Grenoble. Berthet was the son of a Brangues blacksmith. At twenty, he became preceptor in the home of a local dignitary, M. Michoud, and probably became the lover of Mme. Michoud. Leaving the Michoud home, Berthet entered a seminary at Belley, from which he was dismissed as undesirable. From there, he went as preceptor to the home of M. de Cordon. He had an affair with the latter's daughter and was sent away. Now desperate, without a future or position, but still in love with Mme. Michoud, Berthet began writing threatening letters to Mme. Michoud, accusing her of infidelity toward him and of calumny, holding her responsible for his failure. His intimidations and threats finally caused M. Michoud to find a position for Berthet in the home of some cousins. One Sunday, however, Antoine returned to Brangues, followed Mme. Michoud to church, and shot her during the service.

Berthet's story, reduced to this pattern, is the story of Julien Sorel, hero of the novel. The three successive stages in Julien's adventure have their counterparts in Berthet's life. Few details about the third phase of Berthet's life were available from the Grenoble trial records, and Stendhal was forced to stray from the facts in his creation of Julien's experiences with Mathilde in the Mole episode. Critics still debate as to how successfully Stendhal extricated himself from the dilemma resulting from the implicit divergency in the careers of Julien and Antoine in the third phase. (See Commentary, Part II, Chapters 33-35.)

The novel has political and social dimensions also. The story of the individual, Julien, is narrated against a background of contemporary events. A variation of the subtitle given by Stendhal to the novel — *Chronicle of 1830* — calls attention to the circumstances of the composition of the novel and to its political implications. Stendhal conceived the novel at the end of the autocratic reign of Charles X, and although the novelist foresaw the revolution that overthrew the Bourbon dynasty in 1830, he dared not publish it until the following year. (See Commentary, Part II, Chapters 21-23.)

Just as Stendhal's position vis-à-vis his time was one of revolt, his protagonists, as projections of himself, are portrayed as being in conflict with their milieu. Julien Sorel is an outsider, a peasant, nurtured by the example of Napoleon, the army officer become emperor, who would become an aristocrat in a caste society where the equality promised by the revolution was no longer a possibility.

The Stendhalian hero without insuperable obstacles would no longer be a hero, nor for that matter, would he be worthy of portrayal through analysis at all. Since the Stendhalian ideal of the superior man engaged in the elaboration of an art of living to assure him happiness is only conceivable in a negative posture of revolt, society presents itself quite naturally in the role of the obstacle. Julien has not only the exterior world as an obstacle, he is likewise endowed with a contradictory nature that compounds his dilemma. His extreme sensibility, virtue, and generosity will prevent him from succeeding like the unscrupulous, calculating bourgeois parvenu, Valenod.

The novel presents conflict on two levels: Julien's inner struggle is waged between ambition and a predisposition to an idyllic happiness; and his conflict against society engages both aspects of his nature.

The social and political aspects of the novel are inseparably fused with the psychological study of a superior being, and this fusion constitutes the artistic unity of the work. Such an organic unity was lacking in *Armance*.

This novel demonstrates Stendhal's belief that art is the expression of intense emotion, presented with simplicity and directness. The reader, Stendhal hoped, would be jolted by what he read and would participate by visualizing, by experiencing the narration personally. Although Stendhal possessed the extreme sensibility of a woman, as he put it, he reacted violently against the personal effusions and unbridled subjectivity of the Romanticists. He believed that even passion has its modesty. Therefore, Stendhal carefully checks and controls the expression of Julien's emotions as he does his own.

Stendhal's character presentation alternates omniscient analysis and interior monolog. Both methods are characterized by transitional omissions, which betoken Stendhal's "pudeur," his refusal to be penetrated by another consciousness, and by sudden, seemingly spontaneous, affective reactions that startle the characters themselves as much as the reader, and that demonstrate realistically the autonomy of the emotions. These sudden jolts experienced by the characters as they discover themselves and Stendhal's rapid narration create an air of tension that intrigues the reader.

A disciple of the eighteenth-century materialists and a precursor, in this respect, of the determinism of Naturalism, Stendhal conceived the formation of mind and character of man as resulting from experiences he undergoes with external reality. He puts his characters, therefore, in typical situations of everyday life and watches them react.

After the ascension to the throne of Louis-Philippe, the bourgeois king, Stendhal secured an appointment as consul in Civita-Vecchia, Italy, where he served from 1831 to 1836. During this time, he wrote his autobiographies, *Souvenirs d'Egotisme,* the *Vie de Henry Brulard,* and an unfinished novel, *Lucian Leuwen.* These were all published posthumously.

Henry Brulard is just one of the dozens of pseudonyms that Stendhal adopted and discarded during his life. The work investigates his early life through adolescence and was prompted by his need to know himself. It is the antithesis of Rousseau's *Confessions,* in that Stendhal, typically rigorously self-demanding, is frank and truthful to the point of deprecating himself. He reconstitutes his intellectual and emotional formation in Grenoble. Although the work is full of historical inaccuracies, it presents an accurate account of the psychological reactions of the child and adolescent.

The *Souvenirs d'Egotisme* recalls later years, specifically the last years of the Restoration. Stendhal abandoned his autobiographical attempts because of his inability to resolve the inner conflict that they inspired. Although he felt the imperious need to know himself, he was constantly checked by his strong sense of modesty and reserve.

Lucien Leuwen again satirically opposes a protagonist to the contemporary scene, the politically and socially corrupt France of Louis-Philippe. The melancholy and calm of the novel contrast in mood with the tense *Red and the Black.* The hero, Lucien, is not motivated by passion or energy. Rather than imposing himself on the world, he seems to undergo influence more passively, and with aloofness scorns those with whom he must interact. He would seem to exemplify Stendhal's thirst for freedom from restraint. Like Julien, Lucien is in search of an identity and happiness. He is not orphaned or alienated from society, but is protected by his father in a political career, and had Stendhal finished the novel, Lucien would have ultimately married his only love, Bathilde, patterned after Méthilde, and presumably, would have found happiness. In this novel, Stendhal took greater pains to render in depth the lesser characters. His inspiration for the novel went beyond contemporary events. The plot he plagiarized from a work that a friend had written with the request that Stendhal criticize it. Stendhal, no more so than the classicists of the seventeenth century, did not feel scruples about plagiarism.

Temporarily abandoning fiction, Stendhal turned again to biography, *Vie de Napoléon* (1839), to tragic adventure stories, *Chroniques italiennes* (1837-39), and to another travelog, *Mémoires d'un touriste* (1839). The latter is a satire of customs and mores of provincial French life.

Within a period of two months at the end of 1839, Stendhal improvised his second masterpiece in the novel, *The Charterhouse of Parma.* The source was again historical, an old Italian chronicle narrating the life of Alexandre Farnèse. Although the action of Stendhal's novel is placed during the first third of the nineteenth century, the violent passions and fierce individualism of the Italian Renaissance motivate the characters. Love is the theme of the *Charterhouse,* as it had been the major preoccupation of Stendhal's life, although political intrigue and heroic adventures abound.

Fabrice del Dongo follows somewhat the pattern of the Stendhalian hero — he seeks happiness — but in his adventurous pursuit, he is joined and protected by three other chosen creatures. Fabrice does not, therefore, know the social solitude of Julien. He is loved by his aunt, Sanseverina, and protected by her husband, Count Mosca. While imprisoned, Fabrice falls in love with the jailor's daughter, Clélia, and it is this love that changes him profoundly, as it does the other "elect." Fabrice does not repeat the projected denouement of Lucien, however, by an idyllic marriage. Like Julien, Fabrice is allowed but a glimpse of happiness on this earth and he dies young. In Fabrice's separation from Clélia, there is glory and the hope that a final union beyond this life will occur. Rather than being a creature of egotism, such as is Julien, Fabrice is a more generous soul. Even though society is opposed to Stendhal's ideal of individualism, the forceful alliance of these four exceptional beings — Fabrice, Clélia, La Sanseverina, and Mosca — would seem to represent a sort of triumph over society. Balzac commented that this novel could only be truly appreciated by the diplomat, statesman, or man of the world, so intricate are its political innuendos.

Stendhal returned to his consular post in Italy in 1839, where he began his last novel, *Lamiel,* destined never to be completed. Instead of a hero, here he presents a heroine, Lamiel, who further differs from Stendhal's previous protagonists in that she is driven only by an avid curiosity and meets with success by yielding to the expression of spontaneity. She is the most successful adventurer of Stendhal, the most primitive of his protagonists in her amorality, rising from the peasant class to become the queen of Paris.

When Stendhal died in Paris in 1842, his burial in the Montmartre cemetery was attended by three faithful friends, one of whom was Mérimée. Stendhal had written for himself and for the "happy few," and his prediction that he had taken a ticket in a lottery that would be drawn in 1935 has proven accurate, since his most appreciative audience has been that of the twentieth century.

LIST OF CHARACTERS

Julien Sorel

The hero of the novel; peasant son of a provincial sawyer, who, by means of hypocrisy and of the women who love him, driven by insatiable ambition, briefly succeeds in penetrating into the aristocracy. His failure and subsequent death are caused by society's punishment of the parvenu and by the consequences of his own impetuosity.

Mme. de Rênal

Thirty-year-old wife of the ultra mayor of Verrières, and the first and only real love of Julien; she becomes his mistress and through jealousy he shoots her in church. Ultimately, the lovers are reconciled, although she does not long survive Julien's death.

M. de Rênal

Prototype of the provincial petty aristocracy, the ultra, wealthy mayor of Verrières. Blinded by his exaggerated self-esteem, he is the easy dupe of everyone—thus a ridiculous character.

Mme. Derville

Pretty cousin of Mme. de Rênal; one of the happy threesome with Julien and her cousin in Vergy. She helplessly watches her cousin fall in love with Julien, innocently and unknowingly.

Abbé Chélan

Jansenist priest of Verrières, destituted by the intrigues of the Congrégation; first mentor of Julien.

Abbé Maslon

Jesuit priest, tool of the Congrégation, who replaces Chélan as priest in Verrières after the latter's disgrace.

Old Sorel

The crafty, greedy, peasant father of Julien; responsible for his son's unhappy childhood, and at the news of Julien's imminent death, more interested in a possible inheritance than moved by his death.

Abbé Pirard

Jansenist director of the Besançon seminary that Julien attends; old friend of Chélan; Julien's mentor at the seminary, then in Paris: Pirard is instrumental in placing Julien in the Mole household as the marquis' secretary.

Fouqué

Childhood friend of Julien, whose mountain retreat is a refuge for the hero. Fouqué offers Julien a partnership in his sawmill, visits him during imprisonment, and manages his friend's burial.

Valenod

Rênal's assistant and successor as mayor; scheming pawn of the Congrégation; rival of Julien for Mme. de Rênal and instrumental in Julien's death. Prototype of the unscrupulous, bourgeois parvenu.

12

Marquis de la Mole

Peer of France, powerful, ultra aristocrat, who employs Julien as secretary; later treats him as a portégé, and confers nobility on Julien, after the latter has compromised his daughter Mathilde.

Mathilde de la Mole

Impetuous, proud, haughty daughter of the marquis, and second mistress of Julien; after seducing Julien, she becomes pregnant and frantically attempts to save him from the guillotine, although Julien no longer loves her.

Abbé Frilair

Jesuit leader of the Besançon Congrégation; enemy of Chélan, of Pirard, and for different reasons, of the marquis. Mathilde bargains with Frilair to win the freedom of Julien, awaiting trial.

Norbert de la Mole

Son of the marquis; prototype of the colorless, unheroic, conformist young aristocrat of the period. Neither his father nor his sister Mathilde find him worthy of the illustrious Mole ancestry. Julien usurps his role of son of the marquis.

Mme. de la Mole

Wife of the marquis and the prototype of the nullity and sterility of the Restoration aristocracy; holds her court at the Hôtel de la Mole, enforcing an empty decorum and banishing any signs of intelligence and spontaneity; a snob whose only interest is the genealogy of nobility.

Mme. de Fervaques

A prude whom Julien pretends to court to awaken Mathilde's jealousy. She is of Jesuit leaning and of mystical bent. Her bourgeois lineage makes her an uncomfortable aristrocratic parvenue.

Altamira

A liberal, expatriated aristocrat, condemned to die. Julien makes his acquaintance in Paris and idolizes this idealist.

Croisenois

An aristocrat of the ilk of Norbert de la Mole, and his friend; aspires to the hand of Mathilde and dies in a duel defending her honor after the scandal.

Géronimo

Italian singer, bon vivant, adventurer, vagabond; frequents the aristocracy and puts to advantage his social connections.

M. de Beauvoisis

A dandy of the lesser nobility; befriends Julien and serves as a model for the hero in manners and dress.

Prince Korasov

A Russian whom Julien meets in London and in Strasbourg; serves as another mentor for Julien. Korasov, himself a great lover, inspires Julien with the plan to awaken Mathilde's jealousy.

Bishop Agde

Young, successfully arrived, reactionary churchman; Julien serves as his messenger during a religious ceremony of great pomp in Verrières; they meet again at the secret meeting in Paris.

Abbé Castanède

Spy, Jesuit henchman of Frilair. He is a menace to Julien in the seminary and on the secret mission.

Tanbeau

Unsuccessful rival of Julien for the position of secretary to the marquis. Another example of the would-be parvenu.

SYNOPSIS OF THE NOVEL

M. de Rênal, ultra mayor of the small provincial town of Verrières, hires Julien Sorel, a young peasant who aspires to the priesthood, as tutor for his children. The hiring of Julien is calculated to enhance Rênal's prestige among the wealthy liberals. Julien, ambitious and amoral, had hoped to pursue a military career but has decided to enter the priesthood, as the most likely means to success. He chooses hypocrisy as his weapon in his encounter with society. He sees his position as tutor as the first step in his ascension, which will culminate, he hopes, in Parisian aristocracy.

Mme. de Rênal innocently falls in love with Julien after he has lived in the Rênal country home for some time. When Julien discovers that he is loved, he decides that he will seduce Mme. de Rênal, as an expression of the scorn he feels for her husband. His plan of seduction would have failed miserably, so awkwardly does he execute it, were Mme. de Rênal not hopelessly in love with him. Succumbing to Julien's natural charm, which he displays in unguarded moments, Mme. de Rênal becomes, in fact, Julien's mistress. She educates him socially and in the local political intrigues. She succeeds in having Julien awarded a much coveted place in the guard of honor, on the occasion of a visit by Charles X.

Their love affair is idyllic until one of the Rênals' sons falls gravely ill, which Mme. de Rênal interprets as divine punishment for her adultery. Soon M. de Rênal receives an anonymous letter accusing Julien of having seduced his wife. Mme. de Rênal succeeds in duping her husband into believing that the accusation is false. She convinces him that the letter comes from Valenod, Rênal's rival and assistant, who has attempted in the past to court Mme. de Rênal. Her husband believes her because he is comfortably established and is horrified at the thought of a scandal. In order to quiet the rumors, Julien moves into the Rênals' townhouse in Verrières. Because of his brilliant reputation as a tutor, he is invited to dinner by Valenod, who would hope to hire Julien as the tutor for his own children.

A servant girl from the Rênal household, also in love with Julien but spurned by him, denounces the lovers to the former village priest, Chélan, who insists that Julien leave Verrières to enter the seminary in Besançon. Through Chélan's influence with Pirard, rector of the seminary, Julien is awarded a scholarship. Julien's affair with Mme. de Rênal is temporarily ended, but he visits her room for a final rendezvous.

Julien's first attempts to succeed as a student meet with failure because he excels as a scholar, and the Church's reactionary influence that prevails in the seminary requires of its future priests docility and intellectual conformity in mediocrity. Julien's superiority, however, is appreciated by Rector Pirard, who makes Julien his protégé. One day as Julien is assisting in the decoration of the Besançon cathedral, he encounters Mme. de Rênal, who promptly faints at the sight of him.

Pirard obtains a position for Julien as secretary to a powerful aristocrat in Paris, the Marquis de la Mole, to whom Pirard has been of invaluable assistance in a lawsuit. Pirard also leaves Besançon for a comfortable parish in Paris.

Before going to Paris, Julien pays a last visit to Mme. de Rênal, presenting himself at her window late at night. At first rebuffed by his mistress' virtue, Julien artfully destroys her resistance by announcing that his departure for Paris is imminent and that they will never see each other again. Mme. de Rênal acquiesces and Julien remains hidden to spend the following day with her.

Book II finds Julien in Paris as secretary to the Marquis de la Mole. Soon Julien makes his services indispensable to his employer, although his provincial manners and inexperience in high society cause him constant embarrassment. The marquis' proud daughter, Mathilde, takes an interest in Julien when she overhears the latter denouncing the sterility of the Mole's salon. Mathilde is bored with the convention and barrenness of the aristocracy of which she is a part. She is in need of diversion and Julien will provide it for her. The marquis finds Julien's intelligence and wit very refreshing, and ultimately Julien becomes almost a son to the marquis. The latter sends Julien to London on a diplomatic mission in order that he may gain experience and as a pretext to have Julien awarded a decoration.

At the behest of Mathilde, Julien attends a ball, where he makes the acquaintance of a liberal aristocrat condemned to die. Mathilde is the most sought after beauty of the season, but Julien hardly notices her, so inspired is he by the hero he has met. Mathilde, on the other hand, sees in Julien a reincarnation of her illustrious ancestor, Boniface de la Mole, a queen's lover who was beheaded. Mathilde falls in love with Julien.

Julien is unable to decide if he is loved or if Mathilde and her brother and their friends are trying to make of him a dupe. Julien's attempt to leave Paris on a business trip for the marquis moves Mathilde to a declaration of love. Julien, still distrustful, takes precautions to safeguard his reputation, sending Mathilde's avowal to his friend, Fouqué. Alleging another business trip, Julien receives an invitation from Mathilde to visit her in her room late at night. Still convinced that he is being tricked, Julien nonetheless appears at the appointed hour, and after much mutual embarrassment, Mathilde becomes his mistress.

Mathilde now fears that she has given herself a master and she repents of having compromised herself. Julien discovers that he is desperately in love with Mathilde, but her ardor has cooled. Unfortunately for Julien, Mathilde is only capable of loving him when she thinks that she is not loved by him. When in a moment of anger, Julien one day appears to threaten her life, she is in love again. Their second rendezvous occurs, but Mathilde again repents immediately after.

Julien, tormented by passion, is called upon by the marquis to serve as secretary at a secret meeting of reactionary aristocrats and to deliver a secret message to London. Successfully fulfilling his mission, Julien then goes to Strasbourg, where he meets a former acquaintance from London, who advises him how to reawaken Mathilde's love by jealousy. Julien returns to Paris to execute his plan, choosing a prude to court by means of love letters furnished to him by his friend.

Mathilde responds to the stratagem, but Julien realizes that to keep her love alive he must love her at a distance. Mathilde is pregnant, and after the marquis' rage has subsided at the announcement of this news, the latter finally agrees to obtain an army commission for Julien and to encourage his career. Julien occupies his new post in Strasbourg but receives word from Mathilde to return to Paris, that all is lost. In checking on Julien's past, the marquis has learned from Mme. de Rênal, in a letter dictated by her confessor, that Julien is an opportunist who succeeds by seducing women.

Learning this, Julien hurries to Verrières, arms himself, and shoots Mme. de Rênal at church. Imprisoned and awaiting trial for attempted murder, Julien is visited by Mathilde, who attempts to negotiate his acquittal with the Jesuits. Julien is resigned to die and in the solitude of his prison cell discovers that he is still in love with Mme. de Rênal, whom he had only wounded, and that his love for Mathilde has disappeared.

During the trial, in spite of his resolution not to speak in his own defense, Julien informs the court that he is not being tried for attempted murder, but for having attempted to rise above his social class. The jury finds Julien guilty and he is sentenced to be guillotined.

During his last days in prison, Julien finds peace and happiness in his reflections and through the reunion with Mme. de Rênal, who visits him daily. Julien faces death courageously, and after the execution, Mathilde, in a re-enactment of a scene from the Mole family history, furtively steals Julien's severed head and lovingly buries it with her own hands. Mme. de Rênal follows Julien in death.

SUMMARIES AND COMMENTARIES
PART I
CHAPTERS 1-3
Summary

M. de Rênal is the mayor and wealthy owner of the nail factory in the small mountain village of Verrières in the eastern province of Franche-Comté. Situated above the river Doubs, the village owes the prosperity of its peasant citizenry to sawmills and to the manufacture of calico. The sudden arrival of M. Appert, sent from M. de la Mole in Paris to inspect the municipal workhouse and prison administered by M. Valenod, the mayor's assistant, has erupted on the otherwise peaceful existence of the village.

The village, a microcosm of Paris and of all of France in this respect, is politically divided into two camps: royalists like the mayor and a liberal element dissatisfied with the Restoration. They are in agreement, however, upon the importance that they attribute to money and in their slavish respect for small-town public opinion. Father Chélan, Jansenist and village priest for many years, takes M. Appert on a tour of the workhouse and prison, thereby disobeying the wishes of M. Valenod, who risks being exposed for misuse of funds, given the pitiable conditions existing in these institutions. Rênal and Valenod have, in fact, visited Chélan and reprimanded him for this action. This is the subject of the conversation between M. and Mme. de Rênal one day as they are strolling with their three children on the "Cours de la Fidélité," a public promenade sustained by an enormous retaining wall, the glory of Verrières, the construction of which is due to the administration of Mayor de Rênal. The latter then proposes to his wife that they hire Julien Sorel, student priest of Chélan, as tutor for their children, a move destined to increase his own social prestige, since it will cause envy among the liberal textile mill owners. Julien's father, a crafty sawyer, has already, in the past, outwitted Rênal in a land transaction.

Commentary

Note that Stendhal does not rely for his exposition on many pages of description and documentation. His method might be called "free associational" and characterizes the entire novel, since the exposition never ends. It is clearly not that of his famous contemporary Balzac or of the latter's predecessor Scott. (Balzac quite often utilizes the "in medias res" technique of the epic: short dramatic scene, followed by pages of description explaining the initial glimpse, which then re-catches that glimpse and develops it into dramatic narrative.) Stendhal moves rather swiftly back and forth from background description to an action scene as the need arises, after an initial five pages of introductory setting.

Chapter divisions are entirely arbitrary: Chapter 1 situates Verrières, characterizes the economy of the town, then introduces a hypothetical Parisian visitor who will encounter the mayor, giving Stendhal the opportunity to present him for the first time. Most of the short chapter is, in fact, devoted to M. de Rênal, to his home, his past, and his relationship with Sorel, even before Stendhal reaches Chapter 2, which as the title indicates, is to be devoted to M. de Rênal.

Stendhal does not exhaust the description of a newly introduced character upon initial presentation, but rather he returns periodically to "round it out," having been led astray into digressions. Nothing is seen out of relation to other considerations: describing Rênal physically leads Stendhal to ascribe to the passerby a moral judgment about Rênal, condensing time; this then leads Stendhal to Rênal's home; then a parenthetical note about his ancestry; next Rênal's imposing "retaining walls" are evoked; then a comparison with gardens of other manufacturing towns; this leads the author to mention Sorel, since it is through him that the land was acquired; follows a necessary remark about the shrewdness of Sorel; and finally an incident which illustrates that M. de Rênal suspected that he had been bettered in the bargain. Had Stendhal followed the path into Verrières consistently as his means of introduction, the reader would have been enlightened about Sorel's sawmill at an earlier point.

This omission is not an oversight, however. Before Sorel and especially his son Julien, the hero of the novel, can be introduced, the Adversary against which Julien will pit himself in its various forms must be defined. The Adversary will be all of society as it incarnates the corruption and stagnation of the Restoration, thereby oppressing a superior being.

Chapter 1 thus gives us a sweeping, superficial tour; Chapter 2 repeats this gesture, now evoking Valenod and Maslon by the same "afterthought" technique before introducing the action proper: the Rênals' conversation on the promenade. The last few lines of this chapter begin the conversation, the meaning of which escapes the reader, and Stendhal must reappear to furnish more background details at the beginning of Chapter 3. The latter, in turn, involves a "flashback" to an episode having occurred the day before — this before we hear the end of the conversation between the Rênals. Thus, we hear briefly of Julien for the first time in Chapter 3 and we see him through the eyes of M. de Rênal, whose judgment we have already learned to question. Julien can't be a liberal, reasons Rênal, since he has been studying theology for the last three years.

These recurring views of M. de Rênal in interaction with other people permit us to judge him as pretentious, vain, easily duped, proud, and avaricious. Stendhal next turns to Mme. de Rênal and devotes a page to her character and history, taking care to emphasize her virtue and resignation to her lot. She is unaware that life holds anything better than what her husband offers her. Even the method of exposition fits a description of Stendhal's style as that of "improvisation." It suggests the image of ever-widening, superimposed circles.

CHAPTERS 4-5

Summary

M. de Rênal proposes to Sorel the next day that Julien come live with them and tutor their children. Old Sorel, a crafty peasant, meditates the conditions but refuses to answer before he has consulted his son Julien. Returning to his sawmill, Sorel finds Julien reading, sitting astride a beam above the saw he should be tending. Infuriated by his useless son, Sorel brutally knocks the book into the stream. Julien is saddened by the loss of this book, a cherished possession from the legacy his army surgeon friend had left him. His father demands an explanation of the strange offer from Rênal, but Julien is unable to account for it. In solitude, Julien decides that rather than submit to the humiliation of eating with the Rênals' servants, he will run away and enlist in the army. He abandons this plan immediately, however, since it would require that he renounce his ambitions for the priesthood, where success would be certain.

The next day, the bargain is struck, and Sorel has again outwitted Rênal, obtaining as much as he can for his son's services. Julien, meanwhile, has entrusted his possessions—books and military decoration—for safekeeping to his friend Fouqué. On his way to the chateau, Julien judges it wise for his hypocrisy to stop by the church. There he feels his courage waning, but reassures himself with a Napoleonic "To Arms!" and resolutely goes forth to battle in his first encounter at the Rênal home.

Commentary

Stendhal continues alternating exposition and dramatic action in these two chapters. We are not surprised that Sorel outwits Rênal in his two encounters, since we have been prepared for it. Of main interest here is Julien, first seen in his characteristic stance—reading, and in a relatively "high place." This is the first of many times that Stendhal will set Julien physically above his fellows, emphasizing Julien's superiority and solitude and providing him with a secret refuge from society.

The fall from the rafter foreshadows Julien's ultimate fall. He is persecuted then, even by his family because he is different. This aspiring "pariah" will be forever excluded because of his superiority. Note Julien's response to brutality and ugliness: tears. His is a very sensitive nature. It is fitting that Stendhal first presents Julien physically at a moment when he is emotionally moved. Normally pale, his cheeks are flushed with anger, his dark eyes burning with hatred, revealing a reflective and passionate nature. Julien's eternal struggle to control his sensibility by self-mastery and discipline will characterize his future conduct. His hypocritical air helps ward off the blows of his father and will serve as a defense against society.

Julien's dual formation—by the military, through the old surgeon who has inculcated him with respect for Napoleon, and by the Church, through Father Chélan, who has found in him a quick intelligence, readily grasping theology and easily memorizing the Bible—is alluded to in these two chapters, reiterating the novel's title and sketching Julien's situation as representative of the youth of France during the Restoration: born too late to achieve greatness in Napoleon's military endeavors, they must seek it through the Church.

During the interrogation by his father, Julien betrays his pride and ambition in three short, almost automatic utterances: "What will I get for that? . . . I don't want to be a servant. . . . But whom will I eat with?"

We learn that his aristocratic pride is acquired from Rousseau, whose Saint-Preux he also resembles in his extreme sensibility.

Julien's ability to memorize will be an asset both in his success as a preceptor and later, when he plays the same role, that of subservient secretary, but in the highest circle of political intriguers. Another quality of Julien that is sketched is his distrustfulness—of youth, of his peasant heritage. He will not speak to Father Chélan of his new position, since he suspects a trap.

In Chapter 5, Stendhal again takes up Rênal's fear of losing Julien to Valenod—a misunderstanding that will later justify Rênal's blindness to Julien's affair with Mme. de Rênal. It is Sorel who, quite by chance, hits upon the threat of a better offer for Julien elsewhere, which gives the old sawyer the upper hand in his bargaining with Rênal. Mme. de Rênal had already suggested this threat in Chapter 3. On that occasion, Rênal seized the danger as an argument—cleverly contrived, he congratulated himself— for moving ahead with his plan to hire Julien.

The church visit adds to the elaboration of Julien's character, permitting Stendhal to speak of his hero's hypocrisy, his best weapon. This permits more exposition, first of the Congrégation, then of more details of Julien's relationship with Chénal and of his decision to use the priesthood as a means to success. Julien had witnessed the persecution of Napoleon sympathizers and was forced to keep silent on that subject. In alliance with the "ultra" monarchy, the all-powerful Congrégation, a clandestine Jesuit organization, held absolute sway and did not permit dissension.

The art of hypocrisy requires complete self-control. Julien punishes himself for having openly defended Napoleon at a gathering of priests with Chélan. The manner of narration is characteristic of Stendhal: "At one point in the conversation he began fervently to praise Napoleon. He tied his right arm to his chest." Stendhal's psychological analysis sometimes omits transitional thoughts. The causal relationship between the two statements quoted must be supplied by the reader.

A final, very important trait of Julien is his personal honor, his only moral principle. It is called into play when he asks himself in the church if he could be a coward. Here he begins his ritual of self-imposing obstacles which his honor requires that he overcome.

The forewarning that Stendhal intercalates in the form of a scrap of paper (recalling the execution of the historical character who inspired the novel) bearing the ominous warning "the first step" on the other side, cannot be taken seriously by the sophisticated reader. It is simply indicative of Stendhal's penchant for the secretive, the mysterious. Its presence cannot be logically explained, since Julien's fate is realized without recourse to any supernatural powers. It also underlines Stendhal's intention to be closely inspired by reality in writing fiction.

Stendhal turns briefly to Mme. de Rênal, who is having her own doubts about the imminent arrival of Julien. Her initial and ultimate reception of him will be the subject of the next three chapters, so that this final paragraph is transitional.

CHAPTERS 6-8

Summary

Mme. de Rênal receives Julien, and after their mutual embarrassment has changed—for Mme. de Rênal to relief and for Julien to a beginning of composure—he is outfitted in a new suit and presented to the children. Now in complete command of himself, Julien recites at random entire passages of the Bible in Latin, earning the respect and admiration of all. Within a month, he is considered as a real prize by M. de Rênal.

During the next five weeks, Julien engages in petty negotiations beginning his scheme of success through hypocrisy. The self-righteousness that this society feels causes him to feel superior to it, and this, in turn, alienates him from it. His utter ignorance of most matters prevents him, at this stage, from understanding much of what he hears. He craftily convinces Rênal of the necessity of taking out a subscription with the liberal bookseller, presenting the matter in such a way that it will not offend the vanity of the Royalist.

Julien is extremely wary of Mme. de Rênal, since her beauty caused him to stumble when he first arrived. She, on the other hand, is becoming increasingly drawn to this charming and intelligent young man. Unaware of what love is, she gives no thought to the fact that she is attentive to his needs and that her husband is becoming increasingly unbearable to her.

Mme. de Rênal's maid, Elisa, has designs on Julien, and Father Chélan urges him to consider favorably the possibility of such a match and discourages him from entering the priesthood. Julien's burning ardor makes Chélan fear for his salvation should he pursue a career in the Church. Julien retreats, then returns to try to impress the priest by a new tactic. To no avail, for Chélan is not fooled. This is a defeat for Julien.

Mme. de Rênal is overjoyed to hear Elisa confess tearfully that Julien has rejected her. Soon Mme. de Rênal becomes aware that she is in love with Julien.

22

In the spring, the family moves to the summer home in the neighboring village of Vergy. Animated by a fresh outlook, Mme. de Rênal agrees to Julien's suggestion to create a meandering path "à la Julie," among the walnut trees. Catching butterflies provides a new activity and topic of conversation for the inexperienced couple. Mme. de Rênal changes clothes two or three times a day, unaware, however, of what prompts this interest in her appearance. The arrival of Mme. Derville creates a happy threesome. Julien relaxes to the point of reading, not only at night in the solitude of his room but during the day. This increased reading finally gives him some ideas about women.

The three begin to assemble at night outside in the darkness for conversation. One evening, in his animated gesticulation, Julien happens to touch Mme. de Rênal's hand. When it is instantly withdrawn, he decides it is his duty to hold it. A new challenge disturbs his peace.

Commentary

In these chapters Stendhal brings Julien and Mme. de Rênal together for the first time, then concentrates on their separate progression. As will be typical of Julien's character, he reacts spontaneously when surprised by Mme. de Rênal. An aspiring hypocrite must learn to control his reactions. He hates her "because she is beautiful"—that is, her beauty produces a violent reaction in him, a superior being born to exalt in beauty and to be offended by ugliness, but his reaction is spontaneous, and in betraying it, he ruins his "pose."

His pride is offended when she expresses amazement at his knowledge of Latin. Her supplicating tone causes him momentarily to forget his pride, and as his self-confidence becomes progressively stronger, he dares himself to kiss her hand. This daring act he accomplishes. His composure is shattered again when he gives way to the expression of joy, caused by his new clothes, but once again, after collecting himself in his room, he reassumes the calm and dignity befitting a tutor.

The scene relating Julien's arrival is important for several reasons. It establishes the pattern of conduct that will characterize him throughout the novel. In him there seethes a conflict between spontaneous expression of joy associated with happiness and the hypocritical wearing of a mask imposed by ambition. The scene illustrates the tender irony that characterizes Stendhal's attitude toward his "chosen" characters. He deliberately places them in awkward situations that will challenge and embarrass them, after already creating them with a contradictory nature that will cause them to stumble. He has great affection for his "chosen" characters, but he demands of them as much as he demands of himself.

Julien's petty maneuvering wins him minor triumphs in this household which he disdains. Throughout the novel his prodigious memory will be a sure means of winning for him the admiration of others, but it seems to produce a special effect on the provincial bourgeois, incapable, says Stendhal, of appreciating intelligence in any other form. The almost photographic memory that Julien possesses would seem to serve in place of keen reasoning and eloquence to convince the reader of Julien's superior nature, as we will see.

Misunderstanding it, Julien rebuffs Mme. de Rênal's offer of money and succeeds in tricking the mayor on two occasions. His social behavior is quite unacceptable and his efforts to play a role accentuate his ineptness. On the other hand, he unknowingly charms Mme. de Rênal with his eyes. He is unable to deceive Chélan, and the great emotion he experiences at the love and concern shown him by the priest betrays an ardent soul thirsting for friendship and happiness. Thus, to enjoy this emotion completely, Julien takes refuge in the mountains, where his superior soul may not be surprised — unguarded — by the watchful eyes of society.

Stendhal intervenes at this point to assure the reader that Julien will succeed as a hypocrite — he is only a beginner. This intervention betrays the sympathy of the author for his amoral hero and dictates the reader's reaction. Since the novel is also the story of the education of Julien, Stendhal will intervene periodically to praise or censure the conduct of his hero.

For the first time in his life Julien is happy — interestingly enough, only when he momentarily forgets his relentless ambition and hypocrisy. His ambition reawakens at a gesture of Mme. de Rênal: when she withdraws her hand, Julien vows, in a chivalric way, to force her to leave her hand in his. His code of honor is very demanding and depends entirely upon personal criteria. For Julien, personal honor replaces morality.

The chapters advance Mme. de Rênal toward her role as mistress more so than Julien toward his of lover, although the affair will necessarily begin awkwardly and almost by accident, both parties lacking experience and even a conception of what love is.

The awakening and development of love in his characters is illustrative of the crystallization process that Stendhal elaborated in De l'Amour. The feeling manifests itself autonomously of will and, after a preliminary stage of admiration and hope, soon crystallizes in the mind of the lover. This means that it becomes the exclusive obsession of the victim smitten, and every subject, no matter how far removed in appearance, ultimately leads one back to discover new perfections in the loved one.

24

Mme. de Rênal has never before been so deeply moved by a purely agreeable sensation as when she learns that this delightful young man is the stern priest she had anticipated. Note that only when her mind is at ease over the fate of her children does she notice Julien's good looks. She will remain in the early stages of "admiration" for a seemingly long period of time because of utter inexperience and ignorance of love.

She feels in Julien a kindred spirit and she has never imagined that such a man existed, so different from the husband whom she has considered the prototype of manhood. She involuntarily conceals her pleasure at the prospect of Julien's staying, her subconscious forcing the opposite reaction in the conscious.

Mme. de Rênal is greatly moved when she finds Julien beaten by his brothers. She notices the attentiveness that Elisa shows him, then wants to show him kindnesses. Increasingly she disapproves of the lack of delicacy and tact in her husband. Leaning on Julien's arm during a walk, she offers him the gift. His refusal leaves her t embling, and she takes some pleasure in his reprimand. She redoubles her attentions, giving herself the pretext that she has offended him. She becomes physically ill when Elisa speaks to her of Julien's refusal. At this point, Mme. de Rênal becomes consciously aware that she is in love; and what pleasure it is to plead the cause of Elisa, to speak of Julien knowing that he has refused. She actually faints from the joy that the interview causes her. With this realization does not come guilt, since Mme. de Rênal is unaware of what love implies. Thus she plunges head on, in her innocence, attending to her toilette with unprecedented care.

CHAPTERS 9-15

Summary

Julien plans his campaign and, after much anguish, takes Mme. de Rênal's hand the next evening. Although she at first withdraws, he insists, and ultimately, she offers it freely. Rênal offends Julien by accusing him of neglecting the children, but Julien's sullen mood is suddenly changed by the imminence of a catastrophe: Rênal might find his hidden picture of Napoleon as the mayor and the servants change the mattress stuffing. Mme. de Rênal rescues it for Julien, unaware of whose picture the box contains. Rênal, on the other hand, misinterprets Julien's pride for the cunning of the peasant demanding more wages. When he grants Julien a raise, the latter is abashed and scorns the mayor even more for measuring everything in monetary terms. Julien gives expanse to the joy of victory in the solitude of the mountains as he goes to visit Chélan.

The next night Julien dares to show his scorn of Rênal by taking Mme. de Rênal's hand in his very presence, albeit under the cover of dark, and he covers it with passionate kisses. Julien contemplates his campaign against this contemptible bourgeois, while Mme. de Rênal is torn between her jealousy and anguish at the first pangs of guilt, imagining herself to be a fallen woman. Her agitation is so great that she almost betrays her passion by asking Elisa abruptly if it is she, Elisa, whom Julien loves. Mme. de Rênal resolves to treat Julien coldly.

Julien takes offense and does not confide to her his plans to leave for a three-day trip. He stops off again in the mountains to enjoy his freedom in solitude. During their visit, Fouqué offers Julien a partnership that would assure the latter of financial success. After deliberation, Julien rejects the offer, since the success he envisages must be gained through hardship and it must be accomplished by means of the Church. His friendship itself is instrumental in his rejection of the offer. He would not choose to betray Fouqué later, once his education had been financed. Fouqué confides to Julien the tales of his amorous conquests.

Upon his return, Julien discovers that Mme. de Rênal is in love with him, and he decides that his duty requires that he make her his mistress. He announces that he must leave, since he loves her desperately. This avowal sends her into ecstasy, but she innocently assures herself that their relationship will be a platonic one. Julien awkwardly begins his seduction.

His absence caused by another trip to Verrières, where he witnesses the disgrace into which Chélan has fallen, causes his awkward attempts of the previous day to be forgotten. He announces quite abruptly to Mme. de Rênal that he will visit her room at two o'clock in the morning. The declaration is met with an indignant reprimand. He forces himself to carry out this, the most daring of his exploits, and it succeeds only because he forgets his plan and throws himself at Mme. de Rênal's feet. He is unable to enjoy the experience, however, since he is so occupied seeing himself in the role of lover. Returning to his room, Julien's only thought is whether he played his role well.

Commentary

In spite of the obvious earnestness of the characters, the reader cannot help but be amused at the "comedy of errors and cross purposes" that is played out in these chapters, having its climax in Chapter 15 with the seduction of Mme. de Rênal.

This triumph is not due to Julien's art, but rather to his charm, which erupts in unguarded moments; to Mme. de Rênal's love for him, which by this time has become passion; and to the unknowing collaboration of the mayor. Stendhal manipulates the episodes in such a way that each of the three characters acts independently of the others, yet almost by chance they contribute by their convergence to the fortuitous victory of Julien.

This unwitting conspiracy is apparent upon analysis. Julien's ambition to seduce Mme. de Rênal does not result from love for her, but from his sense of duty toward himself. He owes it to himself to take her hand, but he has forgotten the incident the next morning. To motivate this "de-motivated" campaign, Stendhal then utilizes the mayor, whose reproach to Julien for his idleness provokes the latter to avenge his wounded pride by demanding an apology. To the amazement of Julien, the mayor grants him a raise. Julien realizes, however, that this second victory has not been earned, but the elation of the victories must be expressed in the solitude of the mountains.

Julien's next step is again motivated by his scorn for the mayor. What an expression of ridicule to take Mme. de Rênal's hand in the presence of her husband! That evening, Julien relaxes enough to actually enjoy the unknown pleasure that her beauty causes him. Planning his strategy according to Napoleon, he will further crush the mayor by requesting a three-day leave. Already, in spite of himself, however, a feeling for Mme. de Rênal is autonomously manifesting itself. Stendhal comments that Julien longed to see her again, in spite of his expectations. The mutual coldness of their interview summarizes their dilemma: it moves them apart in order, ultimately, to unite them.

The numerous absences of Julien ripen Mme. de Rênal for the ultimate conquest, although Julien does not absent himself for that specific purpose. The tranquility enjoyed by Julien during his second retreat to the mountains is disturbed by Fouqué's offer. Even this obstacle advances Julien's cause, unbeknownst to him: it frees his mind to think of her. Fouqué's amorous affairs teach Julien something about women. Upon his return, therefore, he comes "naturally" to the realization that Mme. de Rênal loves him. This proves to be the greatest step in his progression, since when she herself initiates the hand-clasp ritual, Julien "ups the ante" in his self-imposition of obstacle pattern, deciding that it is his duty to seduce her, to make her his mistress. This decision, then, is made in all lucidity.

With no love yet prompting him, only his ambition and pride, Julien announces hypocritically that he loves her passionately. As he executes his plan, he falls from blunder into blunder, and his attempts at paying court are climaxed by his brutal announcement of the early morning visit he will pay. Had Mme. de Rênal not been moved by Julien's tears of confusion and had her love not progressed to its paroxysm, she would never have given herself. Julien's conquest of Mme. de Rênal and his love for her at this point take the form of a military assault on society.

Mme. de Rênal, on the other hand, already painfully knows the bliss of love. But it has developed in these chapters. She allies herself unknowingly more and more closely with Julien against her husband. The sweet complicity into which she enters with Julien has a twofold importance: it is a sign of a greater degree of involvement with Julien and a means to the realization of a further step in the crystallization of her love because it contains the seeds of jealousy which will torment her.

At first her conflict is between the fear of not being loved and the shame of becoming an adultress. Then when she permits herself to enjoy the thought of happiness with Julien, she is tormented by jealousy, by the fear that he loves another. Soon fear of Julien's departure overcomes any thought she has of resisting him. His hypocritical confession of love for her sends her into a blissful state, although she continues to delude herself as to the future of their relationship, which she can only see as platonic.

The final blunder that precipitates the seduction again reproduces in miniature their entire experience: he clumsily tries to make contact with her foot; she reproaches him, ordering him to be careful; he is offended by the tone and leaves for a day; this absence prepares her to accept him.

In the two studies of love that the novel presents, with Mme. de Rênal, and in Part II, with Mathilde, Stendhal is not only contrasting two types of love—passionate and intellectual—but he is focusing different stages of the love experience, and the two are presented in a complementary way. Julien and Mme. de Rênal are united through blunder and by accident, and separation brings about the union. Julien and Mathilde will both calculate, and Julien will succeed in keeping her love alive only through imposing separation and distance.

CHAPTERS 16-23

Summary

Now their love idyll begins: Julien loves her madly, says Stendhal, but his love is still a form of ambition. Mme. de Rênal's great joy is clouded only by the fear that she is too old for Julien. The second night finds Julien forgetting his role and enjoying his experience. Mme. de Rênal takes great pleasure in educating Julien in social manners and in all the political intrigue that reigns in Verrières, of which Julien has been completely ignorant.

The town is honored by a visit of the king, and Mme. de Rênal succeeds in having a place in the guard of honor awarded to Julien. From his role of dashing, handsome officer, Julien moves to that of attendant priest to Chélan in a religious ceremony honoring the local saint. Other important personages to whose presence his role gives him access are the young

Bishop Agde, officiating prelate, and M. de la Mole, influential and powerful Parisian aristocrat, Peer of France, in the king's entourage.

When one of her sons falls seriously ill, Mme. de Rênal is convinced that God is punishing her adultery. Witnessing her anguish and torment, Julien finds new reasons to love her. When Stanislas is well, her anguish nevertheless remains, since the experience has made her aware of guilt. Their love, however, becomes deeper, more desperate, and somber.

M. de Rênal receives an anonymous letter denouncing Julien as his wife's lover. Julien senses what the letter is and warns Mme. de Rênal not to come to his room that night. She, however, constantly wary that Julien is looking for an excuse to abandon her, comes to his room anyway but is not received. She writes Julien a long letter, elaborating her doubts and reiterating her undying love for him. At the same time, however, she is capable of devising a plan, in the event that there does exist an anonymous letter denouncing them. She will pretend also to have received such a letter, will deliver it to her husband to confound him and to allay his doubts.

M. de Rênal is suffering greatly from wounded pride, anger, and self-pity. He is unable to bring himself to take any decisive step. His wife arrives, hands her letter to him, and in the next breath requests that Julien be sent away for a time until the scandal dies down. This represents exactly the solution Rênal would have wanted. It relieves him of the necessity of finding out the truth, since it is an avowal of innocence on her part. She furnishes him with further evidence in the form of old love letters written to her by Valenod. She succeeds masterfully in putting him on the wrong track, thereby saving appearances and her affair with Julien.

In order to prove to the town that all is well in the Rênal household, Julien lives in their townhouse. There he is visited by the sub-prefect, M. de Maugiron, who, on the behalf of another, sounds out Julien on the possibility of leaving the Rênal household for a new position. Julien congratulates himself on his ability to satisfy Maugiron with a long-winded answer that constitutes, in effect, no answer to his proposition. Invited to dinner at the home of Valenod, Julien inwardly condemns the vulgar ostentation and bad taste of his hosts. When Valenod silences one of the inmates of the workhouse, Julien finds further grounds to feel superior to Valenod and to scorn him. Julien is invited everywhere, he is held in such esteem as a learned and talented tutor.

When the Rênals come for the day to Verrières, mother and children form a happy family group with Julien, and their happiness irks the mayor, who interrupts the scene. The mayor has been forced by the Congrégation to rent out a property at a much lower sum than he could have asked. Valenod, his subordinate whose trickery and intriguing with the Congrégation have brought about the downfall of the Jansenist Chélan, has played a role in this intrigue. Valenod is indebted to the Vicar Frilair of the Congrégation, and at the same time he is ingratiating himself with the liberals, in the event that he falls out of favor with the conservatives and that M. de Rênal takes steps to disgrace him.

Julien learns of these machinations from Mme. de Rênal, and since he attends the mysterious auction, he is taken for the Rênals' spy.

The gloom that reigns in the Rênal household is momentarily dispelled by the unexpected arrival of an Italian singer, recommended highly to Rênal and seeking further recommendations to the French court. His gaiety, exuberance, and talent provide a welcome interlude for the family, and his mission further edifies Julien as to how influence assures promotion and personal advancement.

Meanwhile, several factors precipitate Julien's departure to Besançon. The town is scandalized that M. de Rênal has ignored the talk about the affair in his household. Through Valenod's machinations, Elisa has related to the Jesuit Maslon and to Chélan what is going on between Julien and Mme. de Rênal. Chélan therefore requires of Julien that he either enter the seminary at Besançon, the director of which is Chélan's lifelong friend, or that Julien become the partner of Fouqué. M. de Rênal agrees that Julien must leave. Julien accepts the ultimatum but volunteers, to the great joy of Mme. de Rênal, to return after three days for a last farewell. If Julien goes to Besançon, his education must be financed; if he stays, Valenod will engage him as tutor.

Another anonymous letter received by Rênal presents the occasion for the final intervention of Mme. de Rênal to convince her husband of the necessity of offering money to Julien. At first, Julien accepts the money as a loan, but ultimately, to the joy of the mayor, he refuses it because of his great pride.

Mme. de Rênal, paradoxically, lives only for the last night's rendezvous with Julien, but when it arrives, she is cold and lifeless, anticipating the future emptiness of her life. Julien departs for Besancon.

Commentary

In these chapters, Julien plays a relatively passive role, since his education requires that his experience be enlarged, and this requires that through his teacher, here for the most part Mme. de Rênal, fresh insights into the local political situation be managed for Julien and for the reader. It is as if by seducing Mme. de Rênal, Julien has displayed sufficient initiative so that he may now sit back, without having to play an active role himself. He will have only to feel the effects of his relationship with Mme. de Rênal and of other conditions existing in Verrières.

Besides, this is also a political novel, and Stendhal takes time out to add to his scornful exposé of the evils of the Restoration on the local level.

It is mainly to Mme. de Rênal that the initiative falls because her love has taught her the necessity of ruse. Julien's earlier petty scheming seems even more ludicrous judged against Mme. de Rênal's daring and heroic strategems inspired by love. Her love has crystallized to the point where she would make any sacrifice for Julien: she educates him socially and, at the risk of scandal, obtains for Julien the position in the guard of honor. It is likewise she who takes the initiative to skillfully dupe her husband about the anonymous letters. Their love is that of mother and son, at the same time that it is of mistress and lover. Julien has never had a mother or the love of a family, and Stendhal remedies this lack by the insertion of an idyllic family scene in which Julien displaces completely Mayor Rênal in Chapter 22. The conclusions to be drawn about Stendhal's own childhood are obvious.

Note that it is mainly on faith that we must believe in Julien's superior intelligence, for Stendhal will rarely permit us to witness any examples of his brilliance and articulate eloquence. The author intervenes to assure us of Julien's superiority, others acclaim him (the Valenods and their guests), and Mme. de Rênal herself predicts a great future for such a brilliant man. His inexperience, at this stage, accounts somewhat for the lack of indications, it is true, but in his later experiences in Paris, the same absence of proof will be noticeable. Julien out-jesuits the sub-prefect when the latter attempts to enlist him in the service of Valenod, but we hear none of his brilliant conversational digressions to avoid an answer. Stendhal simply tells us that his reply was perfect, as long-winded as a pastoral letter in that it suggested everything and stated nothing. Since Stendhal was, in a sense, writing the novel for himself and for the "happy few," he evidently felt no need to demonstrate a superiority of which he was convinced. His modesty was another factor in this reticence.

Thanks to the love that Mme. de Rênal has for him, Julien has made two noticeable strides ahead in his onslaught on society: he enjoys a vicarious military experience in the guard of honor, and because of his roles that day, is soon sought after by all of Verrières. He makes progress, profits from his education, in spite of the generally passive role he assumes. He has progressed in the art of hypocrisy: when he lets slip praise of Napoleon and is rebuked for it by Mme. de Rênal, his pride does not incapacitate him, and he is even adroit enough to dodge responsibility for the statement.

Julien's self-appointed role as messenger to Bishop Agde previews his later roles as secretary and as spy. Julien will never attain a position of independence vis-à-vis society, rather he will always be a protected and cherished instrument of others. He actively compares the success of alternative ways of action as he sees them in others. He prefers the refined manners of Bishop Agde to those he has found in the province. He sees everywhere examples of compromise in order to succeed: the letter left in the room occupied by M. de la Mole; the mission of the Italian singer. The latter he compares favorably to M. de Rênal, who is forced to humiliate himself before the Congrégation.

At the Valenod's dinner, Julien is horrified at the ill-treatment the workhouse inmates receive, although he is able to contain his true feelings. In the face of the ultimatum given him by Chélan, Julien debates as to whether he should take offense, but again he remains master of himself, silent in a feigned attitude of humility. It must be reiterated that Stendhal does not condemn Julien's hypocrisy. A nature as sensitive, generous, and spontaneous as Julien's is forced to this extremity to survive.

The playing out of the novel's title in Chapter 18 will not have been missed by the reader: Julien plays alternately the role of soldier, then priest. It will be, of course, the latter vocation that he will choose as a means to success, since Napoleon's disappearance has rendered the former impossible. Nonetheless, the spurs that he wears under the priest's cassock indicate that his career in the priesthood will be marked with the ruthlessness and dashing of the soldier.

Although Julien is capable of more love for Mme. de Rênal than before his seduction of her, he is far from being a victim of it. Goaded by ambition, Julien's mind is not yet a fecund "theater" where this imperious emotion may manifest itself and thrive. Stendhal makes passing allusions to the "mad" love Julien has for her and to the fact that he finds new reasons to love her, but we are hardly convinced. His love for Mme. de Rênal must await the end of the novel for its full development. It might be argued that in making Julien master of the love experience, Stendhal is getting his revenge on all of the women with whom he had been unsuccessful.

Julien's love brings him, at this stage, contentment and a peace and happiness he has never known. He seems to love her more as he sees more and more how much she loves him—particularly when Mme. de Rênal's son is critically ill. At that moment, Julien realizes how completely his mistress is a helpless, suffering victim of love. He feels only momentarily the doubts and torments that continue to plague her and that move her love to constant renewal in new crystallizations. It is quite possible that it is Stendhal's own sensibility, modesty, and need for privacy that prevent him from disclosing much of what Julien's love for Mme. de Rênal entails. For Julien is a projection of what Stendhal would like to be, as are all his protagonists.

It will be obvious to the reader at this point in the novel that Stendhal does not take great pains to conceive an overall view of the action in which subsequent events are mutually interdependent and which would seem to be "necessary" as logical and expected results of previous causes. On the contrary, he invents incidents as he needs them, and the resulting haphazard nature of succession results from an almost improvisational technique of composition and it is one of the meanings of his definition of the novel as a "mirror which is carried along the road."

He needed, for example, the sudden grave illness of Stanislas to permit a further crystallization of Mme. de Rênal's love for Julien and an intensification of his love for her. The unannounced arrival of Géronimo is a fortuitous event needed to alleviate the series of defeats that M. de Rênal has just undergone and that have plunged the household into gloom. In Chapter 23, almost without any warning, the reader learns that because of the scandal of Julien's affair with Mme. de Rênal, a scandal hardly surprising but heretofore not even alluded to by Stendhal, a decision must be made as to Julien's future. Obviously, Stendhal wants to move him on to Besançon, and this is the logical means. Similarly, Elisa chooses this moment to inform Chélan of Julien's conduct, and it is this "father-figure" alone who can prevail on Julien to leave.

CHAPTER 24

Summary

Julien visits the military installation in Besançon before reporting to the seminary. He stops at a cafe, and his fancy is taken by the barmaid, Armanda, who recognizes his obvious embarrassment at the strangeness of this large city. The arrival of one of her lovers nearly incites Julien to challenge him to a duel, but on the insistence of Armanda, Julien leaves the cafe. He stops at an inn to leave his clothes in the safekeeping of the landlady, then courageously starts out for the seminary.

Commentary

This transitional chapter introduces Julien to the city of Besançon, where the next stage of his education will take place. The cafe scene will reappear in the second part of the novel in a slightly different form but producing the same effect. Here, the young, inexperienced country boy ventures into a big city cafe. Stendhal creates for him an almost quixotic episode, where Julien may give heroic proportions to a trivial incident: drawing from his experience as lover, Julien places himself abruptly in the role of Don Juan with Armanda, and his sudden declaration of love to the barmaid is reminiscent of a previous one, pronounced with less sureness but with as much hypocrisy to Mme. de Rênal.

After his brief and audacious visit to the fortress overlooking Besançon, where he has again evoked an imaginary military career, it is here in a cafe that he almost spontaneously gives form to his aggressiveness in an imagined amorous adventure. The arrival of Armanda's lover is but a part of this mock-heroic adventure, immediately awakening in Julien the sense of honor of the knight errant, who, without the intervention of Armanda, would have challenged his supposed "rival." The scenes preliminary to Julien's arrival at the seminary should recall to the reader Julien's visit to the church prior to his entrance at the home of the Rênals. In both, Julien is play-acting, rehearsing, in a sense, for his big scene. He musters up his courage, measures it, or rather "takes its temperature," to assure himself in advance that he will not fall short of the ideal performance required in a new and challenging situation.

Note that the "glance" is the basis of the real and imagined adventure that Stendhal narrates, and he gives Julien almost magical powers of self-extrication. Communication by the "glance" seems to be one of the secretive codes designed to protect the integrity of the superior being.

As was predicted by the priest Chélan, Julien's merit will endanger him because of the envy it inspires in others. Therefore, it is not surprising that Julien seeks protection in women from his enemies. In this short chapter, the two incidents present women as a defense against the world. Lover (Armanda) and Mother (the landlady) are irresistibly attracted to Julien and would protect him.

Even though his method is improvisational, Stendhal relies on "preparation" for the development of plot: this interlude will have served also as the basis of a subsequent plot devised by Julien's enemies to destroy him in the seminary.

CHAPTERS 25-27

Summary

Julien is admitted to the presence of the rector, Father Pirard, by an extremely ugly porter. This impression of ugliness and the fright given by the sternness of Pirard cause Julien to faint. Pirard agrees to give him a full scholarship in recognition of the recommendation from his dear friend Chélan. Julien obviously impresses Pirard favorably by his knowledge of scripture and Latin and by the clarity and insight of his answers. Julien is taken to his cell, where he falls into a deep sleep. His first meeting with Pirard has given him to believe that the seminary is taken seriously by the students. Julien fails miserably in his attempt to succeed by brilliant achievement. He also has erred by requesting Pirard as his confessor, instead of the rector's Jesuit enemy. Julien learns that to distinguish himself and gain acceptance among his fellows he must appear stupid, materialistic, and docile.

The Jesuit Castanède has found Armanda's address in Julien's luggage and has denounced him to Pirard. Confronted by the rector, Julien lies successfully and exonerates himself. It is the baseness, vulgarity, and ugliness of his adversaries—his fellow seminarians—that cause him to flinch and become discouraged in his struggle. His attempts to win them are without success. The description of the ideal awaiting the young priests as preached by Father Castanède revolts Julien: it consists of being well-fed, of vegetating in a parish surrounded by all the physical comforts. His eloquence proves to be another reason for alienation from his fellows, and he must often defend himself against physical attacks.

Commentary

Verrières was protected by walls, figuratively speaking, that Julien succeeded in climbing; now he enters another "prison," the seminary, which he must also conquer. In direct contrast to his imagined conquest of Armanda in the cafe, Julien's interview with Pirard is a confrontation that overwhelms and terrifies him. His sensitive nature shuts out ugliness by rendering him unconscious. Again Stendhal omits Julien's brilliant, concise answers to Pirard's interrogation, although we learn that Julien's answers evoke Pirard's admiration for him.

The keenness of Stendhal's psychological observation is noted in the brief statement occurring at the end of the interview, which casts light on Julien's frame of mind in retrospect: "Julien looked down and saw his trunk directly in front of him; he had been looking at if for three hours without recognizing it." Moments of intense emotional strain prevent us from evaluating objectively a situation except in retrospect.

The prison-like nature of the seminary is emphasized by fleeting views of the outside world, caught by Julien through a window, both during the grueling interview with Pirard and later in his cell. This glimpse of "high places"—mountains, in this instance—serves to reassure Julien, is inspirational to him in this crisis.

Just as Julien blundered in his attempt to seduce Mme. de Rênal, he will blunder in his attempt to succeed in the seminary. The cafe scene served to mark his progress as a seducer, evidence that he had gained experience and wisdom from the experiences in Verrières. Here, however, is a new field of experience, and his evaluation of the interview with Pirard gives him a false sense of security, causing him to fail miserably in his first few weeks in the seminary. He thought that his usual hypocritical mask was the one to assume, but he soon discovers that he has assumed the wrong mask. It is not excellence that is required of the young, would-be priests, rather submission, obedience, and docility. Even in the seminary, Julien is an outsider, a pariah, because of his superior nature. He has great difficulty trying to perfect a mask of stupidity.

Note, however, his progress in the second interview with Pirard. Stendhal admits the reader into a complicity with Julien in the following way: Julien cleverly utilizes the two incidents that had occurred during his first day in Besançon, taking from each what he needs to substantiate his lie to Pirard. Stendhal does not make any comment on this operation. Julien utilizes, then, the potential of Stendhal's logic. Julien's self-imposed campaign of austerity has borne fruits, however, since in not leaving the seminary, he has avoided a worse fate. He has succeeded, again, in spite of himself.

CHAPTERS 28-29

Summary

One priest, however, befriends Julien, Father Chas-Bernard, master of ceremonies of the cathedral. Julien is selected to aid the latter in an important ceremony in the cathedral in Besancon. There he distinguishes himself for his physical prowess and agility in decorating pillars. Here, Julien is also glimpsed by Mme. de Rênal, who promptly faints at the sight of him. He, similarly, is violently moved by this encounter.

Pirard sends Julien as his messenger to the bishop with Pirard's letter of resignation. Julien also learns from Pirard that he is being named tutor in the Old and New Testaments, a signal honor proving Pirard's esteem for him. Contrary to Julien's expectations, the other seminarians accept his advancement as evidence of his merit, that is, they recognize him as one whom they must fear.

Stendhal fills in the political intrigue that has prompted Pirard's resignation: Pirard has allied himself with M. de la Mole in a lawsuit the latter has against Frilair, the powerful Jesuit vicar and organizer of the Besançon Congrégation. Pirard has accepted the generosity of his friend Mole's influence: responsibility of a very wealthy church in the vicinity of

Paris, since he knows that Frilair will succeed in divesting him of his position at the seminary. Julien receives an anonymous gift of money from Mole, who has chosen to honor Pirard's prize student, since the rector himself will not accept recompense for his services in Mole's lawsuit.

Julien receives a wild boar from Fouqué, and this gift further wins the esteem of his fellows, since they believe that Julien's parents have sent the boar and, therefore, must be rich. Julien performs brilliantly in his examinations, but he is tricked by Frilair into displaying his knowledge of Latin poets, poets whose works are banned at the seminary. Julien delivers the letter to the bishop and is invited to dinner. In Frilair's presence he provides a stimulating discussion of the arts for the bishop of Besancon. As a reward, the bishop makes him a gift of the complete works of Tacitus. News of this gift soon circulates in the seminary and adds to the high esteem in which the others now hold Julien.

Commentary

These chapters narrate Julien's success at the seminary. The beginning of Chapter 28 illustrates Stendhal's improvisational technique. The "event" —the protection offered by Father Chas, thus the beginning of his success—needs an introduction to "precipitate" it. The method of having the event happen is Julien's question: Surely among all these learned professors, one at least has noticed my willingness and has been taken in by my hypocrisy?

Julien has overevaluated Father Chas, however. Stendhal. it will be remarked, does not state this fact; the reader must draw the conclusion. Julien is so accustomed to hypocrisy and ruse that he sees it where it isn't. He imagines in this simple priest (the projection in the future of what the materialistically oriented fellows of Julien will become) a very shrewd man with some ulterior motives beneath conversation entirely devoted to revelings in the rich furnishings of the cathedral. In reality, Father Chas-Bernard is only what he appears to be. The priest's disinterestedness gives a certain gratuitousness to Julien's success.

We learn that Pirard is taking Julien more and more into his confidence from his passing warning to the hero concerning his mission into Besancon to aid in the adornment of the cathedral. This isolated note of confidence is a preparation for Julien's future in Paris.

Note again that Julien's physical ascension betokens his aspirations and destiny. He alone is daring enough to risk his neck forty feet off the ground to pose the feathers. The ecstatic reverie that the solemnity of the surroundings inspires in Julien is reminiscent of the scene in Chapter 18 where he watches in ecstasy the ceremony of the ardent chapel. Both scenes betray his highly sensitive, superior nature and contrast his emotional, authentic religious response to the baseness of the Church, no longer a divine instrument, but perverted to political ends during the Restoration.

The unexpected appearance of Mme. de Rênal should not completely surprise us. We know that she has become extremely pious and that, refusing to make Father Maslon her confessor, she frequents the confessional at Besançon. It is also obvious why she comes to Besançon — her passion for Julien is the only justification for her piety. We will find another important encounter between Julien and Mme. de Rênal in a church later in the novel. Her fainting in this scene foreshadows her fate in that later scene, for which Julien will be more directly responsible.

The cathedral episode is the first step in Julien's success at the seminary.

Julien's mentors are kindred souls: noble, of great principle, who have refused to compromise. The austere Jansenist Pirard, just as Chélan, recognizes Julien's nobility of soul and protects him. The touching "communion of souls" that takes place in this scene between Pirard and Julien, two rebels who finally let down their guard and console each other, is reminiscent of Julien's escape sought in high places and solitude in earlier chapters. Note the philosophy of Pirard, similar to Julien's, that has helped to strengthen the latter's character: Pirard has tested Julien by creating insurmountable obstacles in his path. It is Pirard's belief that only the noblest of men could prove themselves by overcoming these obstacles. Pirard tests Julien in this episode, just as Stendhal "tests" his hero throughout the novel.

Julien still interprets incorrectly the attitudes of his fellows. On various occasions during his rapid advancement, he expects hate and receives respect from the seminarians. Stendhal benefits from a certain ambiguity of presentation to maintain the reader's sympathy for Julien. It is uncertain as to how aware of the political maneuvering Julien is; Stendhal chooses not to elaborate this point. It is to be presumed that Julien is as informed as are the others about the rivalry between the Jansenist Pirard and the Jesuit Frilair. The reader is completely informed, however, and our superiority over Julien encourages an indulgent attitude toward his mistakes.

The bishop has no future, and his awareness of this accounts in part for his fair treatment of Julien. He is a power, and independent, but his old age relieves him of the need to intrigue. He is another "father-figure" for Julien, albeit his role is short-lived.

Again, it is by feats of memory, by "bon mots" which we do not hear, and by brilliant discussion, likewise unrecorded, that Julien charms the bishop.

Note the brief allusion to the "Red" in this chapter: Julien is quickly consoled at not being able to enlist as he overhears two old troopers lament the present state of command and the absence of the great Napoleon.

CHAPTER 30

Summary

Pirard refuses to serve as Mole's secretary but recommends Julien for the post. The latter is notified by Pirard to come to Paris but visits Verrières before his departure. Chélan requires that he not see Mme. de Rênal. Julien obtains a ladder, however, and courageously presents himself at Mme. de Rênal's window, not knowing who might be awaiting him there, or how he would be received by Mme. de Rênal. She admits him with reluctance; and after three hours of conversation, he succeeds in overcoming her remorse. She has given herself with a certain gaiety and abandon, an attitude that she retains the next day while she hides Julien in her room and, in spite of endless perils, until the next night. The arrival of M. de Rênal, who has discovered the "thief's" ladder, pounding on her door, causes Julien to leap from her window and to take flight to Paris, on the road to Geneva, however, to avoid capture.

Commentary

It is obvious that Pirard's journey to Paris is a means to get Julien there, and with a position, that is, protected by the powerful M. de la Mole. Julien can only assume that the gift he has received comes from Mme. de Rênal. The superiority of the reader invites our complicity with Julien's other mentors. It is fitting that Julien returns to Verrières before undertaking the next stage in his education in Paris. We are thereby made more aware of the distance covered in his formation. Fourteen months have passed, we are told, but we are not noticeably aware of the passage of time with Stendhal. We have, rather, the impression of a non-ending present. Contrast Julien's attitude as he undertakes with premeditation the seduction of Mme. de Rênal to his awkwardness on the first occasion. A refusal on her part would have been a disgrace for his honor, and he is forced to cold calculation to overcome her remorse. The ruthlessness with which Julien calculates this seduction shows us the extent to which the hypocrisy of the seminary has permeated his character. His threat to leave and the avowal that he will be going to Paris never to return force her consent.

Note the means employed by Julien to gain access to Mme. de Rênal's room prior to their last meeting. It is possible that Julien recalls his meeting with Mme. de Rênal in the Besançon cathedral, a scene in which he had utilized a ladder to perform another act of daring: the decoration of the church. Stendhal flatters the intelligence of his reader by not making explicit this associational mechanism in the mind of Julien. In both incidents Julien distinguishes himself by a spirit of adventure, a necessity to engage his entire existence in a single act, regardless of the consequences.

What of Julien's love for Mme. de Rênal? Once again he is able to appreciate her greatness of soul as he witnesses her courage and gaiety in the face of danger. They are worthy of one another in their heroism. The dangers to which his visit exposes Mme. de Rênal, both real and in the form of remorse which will no doubt follow, and Julien's insistence —everything indicates that although Stendhal says that Julien "adores" her, his love is rather a need to be loved, to be preferred, to be the object of sacrifice for another.

PART II

CHAPTERS 1-4

Summary

Julien's voyage to Paris is enlivened by the conversation of his fellow travelers—a Bonapartist, former friend of M. de Rênal, and a newly formed liberal, Saint-Giraud, who is fleeing the pettiness and intrigue of provincial life for the calm of Paris. The latter had sought peace in the provinces, but because he refused to take sides in the great debate between ultras and liberals, he was persecuted by both. The conversation reflects their opposing political views: Saint-Giraud maintains that the present disorder is due to Napoleon's desire to revive the monarchy. Such strong argumentation does not prevent Julien, upon his arrival in Paris, from making a pilgrimage to Napoleon's palace at Malmaison.

Pirard describes to him in detail the new life he will lead at the home of the Marquis de la Mole. Pirard warns Julien of what to expect from this aristocratic and haughty family.

Chapter 2 is devoted to Julien's arrival and few days in the Mole household. He is first presented to the marquis, who has him outfitted and finds it necessary, in order to improve Julien's grace, to have him take dancing lessons. Invited for dinner in the salon, Julien meets Mme. de la Mole and Mathilde. The latter he finds uninteresting and even unattractive, in comparison to Mme. de Rênal. He finds Norbert, the marquis' son, charming. At dinner, Julien succeeds in making a favorable impression by his knowledge of the classical writers.

Julien takes his working post in the library, where the vast array of books dazzles and inspires him. Mlle. de la Mole enters to smuggle out a copy of Voltaire, and this encounter strengthens Julien's impression of her as a cold-hearted, uninteresting woman. Norbert, on the other hand, continues to delight Julien by his kindness, and he accepts Norbert's invitation to go riding. A mishap while riding is later related at dinner, and Julien's good grace and innocence in the avowal of his awkwardness cause the marquis to look favorably upon him and incite the curiosity of Mathilde.

Further equestrian attempts on Julien's part elicit the remark from Norbert at dinner that Julien is very courageous. Julien's many mishaps are especially relished by the servants of the household.

Chapter 4 describes a typical evening in the salon of the Mole family. Julien reacts as violently to what he witnesses as he did in the Verrières home of Valenod, and the scenes are, in fact, similar. Court at the Mole's is strongly reminiscent in its sterility of the court of Louis XVI. There reigns an air of decorum, politeness, and cruelty. Only insignificant subjects are discussed, nothing controversial, and the barrenness of the conversation inevitably leads to calumny, derision, and mockery, by those in favor with M. de la Mole, directed at those out of his favor. Admitting to Pirard how distasteful he finds these evenings, Julien is overheard by Mathilde, who admires this courage and sincerity.

Commentary

Stendhal loses no opportunity to further the education of Julien, rendering, at the same time, a view of the political situation of the period. Julien would seem by nature and inclination to be a liberal, although he frequents only ultra milieus: the Rênals and the Moles. Julien is, in fact, an opportunist—he has no allegiance, except to himself and to others of the "happy few" who befriend and love him. The only reaction that Julien registers at this revelatory discussion during the coach journey is one of astonishment, and Napoleon remains his idol.

Saint-Giraud's situation is an ironic preview of what Julien's future holds, but in reverse. Saint-Giraud is returning to Paris, after having vainly sought peace in the provinces. He apparently considers Paris as the lesser of the two evils. Julien will follow the reverse route—arriving at the same conclusion: present happiness is not appreciated.

The scene is an effective transition between the scenes of action from another point of view. It indicates that France's lamentable situation during the Restoration is localized neither in Paris nor in the provinces—it is ubiquitous. We have seen corruption and compromise as it operates on the local level, in the grass-roots, then in the seminary, where the purveyors of weakness are formed. Now we will witness the motor source of France's sickness in the aristocratic and ecclesiastical powers in Paris.

Note the father-function of Pirard, whose kind intervention will minimize Julien's chances of being ridiculous in the Mole household.

Although the other members of the Mole family are cruelly and concisely described by Pirard, Mathilde is only briefly mentioned at this point.

Compare Julien's wary but self-assured air upon introduction to the Mole household to his awkwardness and intimidated state upon arrival at the Rênal home, fifteen months before. Stendhal tells us that Julien has come to expect the worst from people; therefore, he is not easily intimidated.

Note, however, how astutely Stendhal renders, almost in passing, a psychologically convincing detail describing Julien's manner of confronting a new situation, where he must find some weakness in his adversary, the discovery of which will bolster Julien's own confidence. (The same mechanism functioned for Julien as he met Mme. de Rênal, whose beauty had intimidated him.) It seems to Julien that M. de la Mole's wig is much too thick. Thanks to this observation, he is not at all intimidated. That is, observing no matter how slight a deficiency in a superior, Julien is able to derive confidence from it. At dinner, his self-assurance does not falter, this time because he decides that Mathilde de la Mole will never be a woman in his eyes.

Mathilde takes an interest in Julien for the first time in Chapter 3, and it is his uniqueness and candor, in contrast to the stereotyped characters to whom she is accustomed, that will constitute much of the basis of her interest and subsequent love for Julien.

Julien must undergo a social metamorphosis as part of his education, and learning to ride a horse is part of this training. Stendhal notes, at the end of the chapter, that Julien already feels himself to be an outsider in this family, the customs and manners of which are strange to him. This concluding remark serves as a transition to the subject matter of the following chapter.

Stendhal benefits from Julien's role of outsider to view the sterility of this social institution, the aristocratic salon of 1830. Pirard's austere presence and conspicuous isolation contrast with the habitués' obsequious conduct, their superficial and docile character, as they mingle and assume their roles in their respective sub-circles. Julien does not fail to note this contrast. Julien's violent disapproval of the cruel derision of merit, especially by his rival secretary, Tanbeau, is reminiscent of his reaction at the Valenod's dinner party. It is by means of this device that Stendhal elicits the reader's sympathy for his hero: Stendhal satirizes Julien's adversaries through ridicule; the reader, therefore, naturally allies himself with Julien.

Admitted as a silent spectator into Mathilde's circle, Julien observes her suitors, the most favored of whom is the Count de Croisenois. In passing, Stendhal observes that Mathilde admires Julien's courage in denouncing this type of social gathering to Pirard—a second hint at the future relationship of Julien and Mathilde. The description of the salon no doubt inspired Proust in his own vivid and satirical depiction of early twentieth-century salon mores. It was Proust, incidentally, who first called attention to the recurrent theme of "high places" in the works of Stendhal.

CHAPTERS 5-7

Summary

After several months, Julien has made his services very valuable to M. de la Mole, although, socially, he has fallen from favor in the household. He applies himself tirelessly to his work, and to escape the discouragement that his exile causes him to feel, he devotes his leisure time entirely to fencing and riding. Norbert is estranged from him, and Mme. de la Mole finds Julien's impetuosity and sensitivity repugnant to decorum.

Julien is offended by a rude individual in a cafe one day, and he immediately challenges the man to a duel. Going the following morning to the address indicated on the offender's card, Julien finds, to his surprise, that the Chevalier de Beauvoisis, whose name is on the card, is the master of the coachman who had offended Julien. Julien promptly punishes the coachman for his insolence, and the chevalier agrees to a duel. Julien is slightly wounded, but the new acquaintance soon becomes friendship. The chevalier is a model aristocrat whom Julien imitates in manners and attitude, accompanying him to the opera. In order to escape the ridicule that would result from public knowledge that he had dueled with a sawyer's son, the chevalier spreads the rumor that Julien is the natural son of a close friend of the Marquis de la Mole. The latter, upon hearing this rumor, is greatly amused.

Bedridden with gout, the Marquis de la Mole is reduced to the company of Julien during the absence of his family. The marquis discovers in Julien a man of ideas and of quick wit. The marquis makes Julien a gift of a blue coat, and when Julien visits him in the evenings wearing the garment, the marquis treats him as an equal. Julien introduces efficiency into the marquis' business affairs, and his innovations are so much appreciated that the marquis wants to reward him with a gift of money. This Julien declines, pretending that the gift would ruin the relationship with the man in blue, since it is to that man and not to the man in black that it is made.

Recognizing the inborn nobility of Julien, the marquis devises a plan to confer upon him the cross of the *Légion d'Honneur*, which will constitute an exterior acknowledgment of Julien's inner nobility. He sends Julien to England, where he is introduced to various notables in the highest circles. Upon his return, Julien is told that when he wears his decoration, he will be, in the eyes of the marquis, the son of the Duc de Retz, a friend of the marquis. The decoration makes Julien more confident.

A visit is paid to Julien by Valenod, recently made a baron. Valenod has replaced Rênal as mayor of Verrières. Ironically, Valenod was the ultra candidate, and Rênal the candidate of the liberals. The marquis agrees to receive the mayor and intends even to encourage his political career. Benefiting from his more intimate relationship with the marquis, Julien succeeds in having his own father named director of the workhouse and Cholin named as director of the lottery. Julien learns later that his intervention has thwarted the candidacy of an honest man, M. Gros, who, Julien recognizes, really deserved and needed the appointment to the lottery post. This causes Julien some remorse, which is quickly stilled, however, by a rationalization that expediency sometimes brings about injustice.

Commentary

These chapters constitute a further stage in the education of Julien, specifically as the protégé of M. de la Mole. Chapter 5 is preparatory to the subsequent development of the father-son relationship, in that it points up Julien's success and failure: success as a prized secretary; failure as a social creature in this blasé aristocracy in which he moves.

Note again Stendhal's tenderly ironic treatment of his hero in the cafe scene. Stendhal will make a fool of Julien by exploiting his hero's basically contradictory nature, causing his impetuosity to play out another mock-heroic adventure. Julien is "unmasked" by a less glorious counterpart: the "gentleman" whom he challenges turns out to be a lackey, like himself. Typically, however, Stendhal takes care not to exploit the ridiculousness that would be inherent in such a situation. Stendhal permits himself to make light of Julien, delicately, but the reader may not take this liberty. The same restraint is apparent in the handling of the encounter with the chevalier. Instead of taking offense, the latter, another of the "happy few," befriends Julien and plays the role of fairy godfather.

Stendhal calls to our attention the resemblance between the two café scenes. He utilizes repeatedly the recurrence of similar situations at different points of the narration, and such a device is particularly effective in a novel describing the formation of an individual. An event that repeats itself calls our attention to the distance covered by the character. In this instance, we note that Julien's pride has not weakened but that he is now more highly placed on the social ladder.

The duel episode serves also to further the relationship between Julien and the marquis. The rumor of noble but illegitimate birth circulated by the chevalier "suggests" to the marquis, without his own awareness of it, the action he takes to confer a kind of nobility on Julien in Chapter 7. By the end of Chapter 6, the fatherly interest felt by the marquis in Julien has progressed to the point where the marquis wants actively to "form" his secretary. Hence, he stations Julien at the Opéra to study another spectacle, the impressive entry and departure of the aristocracy, in order that Julien may imitate their ways and rid himself of his remaining provincialisms.

Betraying his negligence in plot manipulation and preparation, Stendhal feels obliged, in Chapter 7, to justify the familiar tone in which the marquis has just addressed Julien at the end of the preceding chapter. Such an intervention Stendhal would no doubt justify by evoking his realistic pretention and his definition of the novel—he is not inventing, he is only reporting the truth, and this detail he had forgotten to mention. Stendhal indicates to the reader to what extent Julien has actually replaced Norbert as a worthy son for the marquis, both in the eyes of the latter and in those of Stendhal.

"Play acting" recurs as a theme in these chapters, and the deliberate insincerity that it implies is a necessary quality of the nobility to which Julien aspires. The marquis, another fairy godfather, intervenes as for Cinderella, outfitting Julien and casting him in a dual role. A truly noble soul is capable of effecting metamorphosis by will. Thus, the marquis is "magically" empowered to transform Julien into the gentleman in the blue coat by night and into the black-coated secretary by day.

That Julien is making progress is obvious by the fact that he surpasses his master's performance. By proudly refusing the well deserved gift, Julien intimates that the marquis is violating the rules he has established himself. This performance inspires the marquis to bring about the next transformation: Julien's diplomatic mission to London, which will serve as a pretext for a decoration. Julien's frequenting London's high society is the culminating phase in the stage of his formation related in these chapters.

Valenod's reappearance and his victory over Rênal serve to remind the reader of the changing fortunes on the political scene. Valenod's ascendancy had been predicted in Chapter 1 of Part II. Stendhal is careful to note that antipathy and rivalry still exist between Julien and Valenod. This fact will be utilized in the ultimate determination of Julien's fate.

The close of Chapter 7 reminds us that Julien's experiences have taken their toll on his principles and innocence. In short, he is being corrupted but, fortunately, this change is reversible. In the incident in question, Julien has occasion only to rationalize his remorse. One cannot help but wonder which would have won out, expediency or principle, had Julien known earlier that Gros was also aspiring to the position in which Julien's intervention has established Cholin.

CHAPTERS 8-9

Summary

Julien sees Mathilde after a period of separation, and she commands him to attend a ball with her brother. Julien is dazzled by the magnificence of the Hôtel de Retz and by the brilliance of the aristocracy in attendance. Although Mathilde is the center of attraction, she is bored with the lack of color that characterizes all of her suitors. Julien and Altamira, a liberal condemned to die, are the only men present who intrigue her, and they seem unmoved by her charm, unlike Croisenois and the others of his ilk.

In her boredom and because of her fascination with the unconventional, the exciting, the unusual, Mathilde seeks out the company of Julien and Altamira, who are deeply engrossed in a conversation about political expediency and idealism. They remain oblivious to her presence. Piqued, Mathilde seeks to tire herself by dancing and engages in a verbal bout with the impertinent Fervaques, a bout in which she is pitilessly victorious. Julien's admiration for Altamira is unbounded, and the day after the ball, as he works in the library, he is still engaged in an endless inner debate between expediency and idealism. Mathilde appears and reappears, hoping to attract his attention. When Julien deigns to answer her question about the object of his thoughts, he overwhelms her with his reflections. Mathilde hastily retires, realizing that she has interrupted his thoughts.

Commentary

These chapters serve as preparation for the beginning of Julien's affair with Mathilde. Unaware that she is doing so, she will instinctively seek out Julien, as a potential realization of the ideal she seeks—a noble soul, capable of self-sacrifice for great ideals.

The chief point of view of narration is that of Mathilde. Stendhal's artistry as a psychological novelist requires that the reader supply the explicit formulation of the characters' motivation. Why does Mathilde command Julien's presence at the ball? We are to conclude that this is precipitated by her boredom and by the conversation she has had with her father concerning Julien. In that conversation, the marquis praised Julien for being capable of the unexpected and found his own son inferior by comparison. Stendhal transforms psychological analysis into action, expecting the reader to supply the explicit description of the psychological movement. Not even Mathilde arrives at an awareness of her own motivation.

Stendhal creates the ball, in all its sterile glitter, as a fitting stage where Mathilde's boredom may be displayed as having reached its paroxysm. In this regard, the ball scene is the culmination of the salon scenes in the Hôtel de la Mole.

Stendhal takes little interest in describing the ball as such. He presents no exhaustive description of costumes, physical surroundings, or of guests. We have the impression of crowds mainly because Mathilde seems endlessly searching for Julien. Stendhal limits the point of view to that of Mathilde and Julien. The reader's appreciation of the ball is, therefore, limited to that of the characters. This represents a partial abandonment of the traditional omniscient point of view and previews more radical innovations in technique by late nineteenth- and twentieth-century novelists.

Were Mathilde less appealing to her suitors, she would be less bored. Stendhal emphasizes her role as the most sought-after beauty of the season in order to put her boredom in relief. Any unearned victory, rather victory as such, is considered by Mathilde as a defeat, since it supposes an end to battle. Happiness, for the "beyliste," is no more than the search for happiness. Ironically, only those potential realizations of Mathilde's ideal are indifferent to her—Altamira and Julien.

It would be inexact to say that Mathilde is, at this stage, directing her attentions exclusively toward Julien as an individual. Julien and Altamira appear, not as individuals, but as a human type, a realization of her ideal. Mathilde's ideal will ultimately individualize itself into Julien.

Julien finds a kindred soul in Altamira, the only individual in the novel who earns the hero's unreserved admiration. In these chapters, Stendhal gives more ample consideration to the conflict between idealism and expediency. Ironically, Julien aspires to revolutionary liberalism, but he is becoming more firmly entrenched in the home of an ultra. He, an ambitious pariah, idolizes Altamira, a liberal whose idealism has condemned him to death. This, Stendhal is saying, is the lamentable state to which the glorious revolutionary principles have degenerated during the autocratic Restoration. Altamira is Julien's double. Because of her pride and superiority, Mathilde is very worthy of Julien, although he continues to find her unattractive, and her pride offends his. Julien has become a dandy, Stendhal tells us, and he conducts himself coldly as a defense against Mathilde's haughtiness. He will not fail to notice, however, that others admire her, that, in fact, she is the attraction of the ball. He will begin to see her differently, since prized by others, she must be worthy. Note that Julien disagrees with Altamira, although the reader realizes that Julien is really undecided as he defends so forcibly the position of expediency.

The graphic image of character disposition that may be seen in the ball scene is the following: Altamira is impassioned by his ideal of freedom; Julien shares this ideal and is only attentive to its exponent, Altamira; Mathilde instinctively pursues both as representatives of her own heroic ideal. The result, temporarily, is parallel and unfulfilled aspirations.

CHAPTERS 10-12

Summary

As Julien's ardor cools, he is able to reflect on Mathilde's attitude toward him, and he begins to see her in a new light. The academician tells Julien the story of Boniface de la Mole, ancestor of Mathilde, who was beheaded in the Place de Grève defending his friends, and whose lover was the Queen Marguerite. The latter heroically retrieved Boniface's head and lovingly buried it. Mathilde reveres this ancestor and wears mourning on the anniversary of his death. This knowledge evokes Julien's admiration for Mathilde, and in subsequent conversations with her in the garden, he finds that she is intelligent and charming. Finding himself treated kindly by Mathilde, Julien wonders whether she loves him. Then his suspicious nature sees a plot being perpetrated by Mathilde and her brother to make him look ridiculous. Julien decides to seduce her, then to flee. He is tormented by the suspicion that she loves him. Mathilde, on the other hand, has arrived at the discovery that she must be in love with Julien.

Mathilde praises Julien in the presence of her brother, Caylus, and Croisenois, and, to their surprise, ridicules them in Julien's defense. She attributes their condemnation of Julien to the jealousy they must feel for a man of genius. One evening, Julien hears his name mentioned in an argument between Mathilde and her brother, and when he joins them, silence falls, and Caylus, Croisenois, and de Luz treat him coldly.

Commentary

Julien discovers immediately how to have a successful relationship with Mathilde. He must remain cool and never permit her momentary sympathy to lull him into complete confidence. He notices that their conversations seem to begin as a duel, and he realizes that, in order to command her respect, thus her admiration, he must maintain a certain distance between them. Later, as their relationship becomes more involved, Julien will forget this discovery momentarily. His ultimate success with Mathilde will depend upon his rediscovery and utilization of this strategy.

Julien is still master of himself. He suspects that Mathilde loves him, but he is not the victim of any passion for her. Here reawakens the peasant's distrust and suspicion. Julien's fear of ridicule (a trait of Stendhal's heroes) conflicts with his growing admiration for Mathilde, and the resulting decision to seduce her indicates the victory of his suspicious nature. According to Stendhal's theory of love, some assurance and encouragement that one is loved are necessary before one's own feelings progress in the crystallization process.

Chapter 11 is an exploration of Mathilde's character and presents the culmination of the various preoccupations she has had since Chapter 8. Stendhal describes typical incidents that illustrate her pride, the command she has over others, her boredom with the ordinary; and he continues the self-analysis she made at the ball. Mathilde arrives at the discovery that she must be in love with Julien and is overjoyed at this prospect. In reality, she is in love with the idea of being in love. Hers is a love in the Cornelian sense: it depends upon her intellectual approval of it, and it is necessary that the object of the love prove himself worthy of it. She projects its future course: "I've already shown boldness and greatness of heart by daring to fall in love with a man so far below me in social position, I wonder if he'll continue to be worthy of me. At the first sign of weakness I see in him, I'll abandon him."

Chapter 12 is but the continuation of the preceding, in that Mathilde continues to subject her love for Julien to cold intellectual analysis. She rationalizes it, justifies it, and revels in it. Here for the first time, Mathilde verbalizes the association between Julien and herself and Boniface and Marguerite, an association she has unconsciously forged since Chapter 8.

Mathilde has arrived at that stage in crystallization in which every virtue and perfection is attributed to the object, once the realization of love has come to awareness. She sees Julien as a superior man who despises others, and that is why she doesn't despise him. Doubtless, she defends Julien with greater vigor because of the overwhelming disgust that her brother and suitors inspire in her, as the epitome of the commonplace. Even Norbert's warning that Julien is a future revolutionary who would see them to the guillotine is simply another reason for Mathilde to love him. What does worry her, however, is the possibility that Julien does not love her. At any rate, Mathilde has escaped her boredom by deliberating about this decision to indulge in a great passion.

Julien still wavers between his doubts and hopes concerning Mathilde's intentions. In this respect, Julien would seem to be experiencing a variation of the crystallization process, although Stendhal's modesty prevents him from showing Julien as a victim of this emotion.

CHAPTERS 13-16

Summary

Julien finds himself in love with the beauty and charm of Mathilde, and even his previous, black vision of her as a Catherine de Medici forms part of the ideal she is becoming for him. Convinced, however, that he will be made a dupe, Julien pretexts a business trip to Mole's estates in the Languedoc. This threat of departure moves Mathilde to action, and in the declaration of love that she writes him, she states that it would be beyond her strength to be separated from him.

Julien is overjoyed at this avowal and convinces Mole that the latter's affairs in Normandy now require a change in plans and Julien's presence in Paris. Mole's joy at Julien's plans causes a conflict to rise for Julien. How can he seduce the daughter of a man who has been so kind and who is so attached to him? He silences this scruple and, still driven by his mistrust of these aristocrats, devises a plan whereby, if need be, there will exist proof of Mathilde's attempt to seduce him. He copies the letter, sends it in a Bible to his friend Fouqué for safekeeping. Then he composes a truly diplomatic letter as an answer to Mathilde, an answer that does not compromise him.

Mathilde writes Julien a second letter, impatiently demanding an answer. Julien complies, but admits nothing and announces his imminent departure from Paris. In order to deliver it to her, he strolls in the garden, and there he catches her eye as she watches him from her room. The next exchange contains her queenly command that Julien is to come to her room by means of a ladder at one o'clock.

The evening before the rendezvous finds Julien still debating over Mathilde's intentions. Prepared for the worst, Julien imagines the various

50

means at the disposal of the conspirators to capture, murder, and disgrace him. He sends more copies of Mathilde's letters to Fouqué, together with a sealed denunciation to be circulated to various newspapers in the event of a catastrophe. Julien tries, in vain, to read betrayal on the face of the servants and of Mathilde during dinner. He strolls in the garden, wishing that she would appear to reassure him. He then reproaches himself for having stooped to ingratitude that would compromise the honor of such a noble family. He regrets having mailed the letters to Fouqué.

At the appointed hour Julien climbs the ladder to Mathilde's window. Their first moments of conversation are forced, and both are very ill at ease. Julien stealthily inspects the premises, searching for concealed enemies. Finally he confesses his suspicions to Mathilde. They search desperately for subjects of conversation. Julien's evident assurance as he projects future meetings causes Mathilde to realize with horror that she has given herself a master. After much hesitation, Mathilde decides that she owes it to Julien, who has displayed much courage by appearing, to give herself to him. Neither finds pleasure, however, in the act of love. Julien departs before dawn, riding to the heights of Meudon, where at last he finds happiness. Mathilde asks herself whether she loves Julien, after all.

Commentary

These chapters relate the development, manifestations, and expressions of the duel of love that is waged between Julien and Mathilde. Chapter 16 culminates in the first rendezvous in her room, representing a definitive victory for Julien. Although Julien has certainly been formed by the action since his days in Verrières, his success with Mathilde depends on his own blundering, which is reminiscent of his affair with Mme. de Rênal. It is his distrust, his suspicion that he will be made a dupe that prevent him from accepting Mathilde's overt advances. This coldness, on the other hand, is exactly what encourages Mathilde, and her fear of losing Julien prompts her to make the first written avowal. In spite of Stendhal's ironic treatment of the lovers' dilemma, Julien remains the fictitious Stendhal who coolly puts into operation what Stendhal himself had learned about the mechanism of love, as expressed in *De L'Amour*.

As it has been shown, Julien is vaguely aware of the uniqueness of the psychology of this haughty Mathilde, but he is unable yet to exploit his knowledge efficaciously. The element of gratuitous victory is also present in his evaluation of her character. He sees her as machiavellian, exaggerating her duplicity. She is, in fact, complex and strange, but not in that way. He is, therefore, right and wrong simultaneously. Stendhal gives to Julien an awareness of his own crystallization process. Julien attributes to Mathilde all qualities; he imagines her to be Catherine de Medici. "Nothing was too profound or too criminal for the character he ascribed to her." Julien, like Mathilde, seems to be in love with an ideal. Mathilde is undergoing the same torment, fearing that Julien feels nothing for her. The theme of self-delusion, manifest here in the area of love, is one of the dominant Stendhalian themes and constitutes part of his uniqueness as a psychological novelist.

The rationalization that Julien makes of the affront of which he is guilty toward M. de la Mole is a very convincing demonstration of the title of the novel. Julien vindictively shouts his battle cry: it's every man for himself in this desert of selfishness known as life. Why should providence have given him such a noble soul and not the material success that should accompany it? He has been denied the brilliant uniform that Croisenois wears, but he has known how to choose the uniform of his time—the priest's cassock that could ultimately become a cardinal's robe. Julien sees the necessity of a strategic campaign, cloaked in duplicity, as the only means to success. He begins the attack by composing his diplomatic letter to Mathilde.

Chapter 14 illustrates again Stendhal's concentric-circle technique of narration. He now returns to a description of the circumstances surrounding the delivery of the first letter to Julien, this time from Mathilde's point of view. Like Julien, Mathilde has undergone a conflict as her love has progressed. She has feared that she is not loved, and the new fear is born, to become stronger later, that she has given herself a master. Stendhal then shifts to Julien's point of view, proceeding to the second and third letters from Mathilde. Still undecided as to the reality that confronts him, Julien plans for both eventualities: either Mathilde's love for him, regulated by her pride; or the comedy in which his adversaries would make him the dupe. He realizes that he made a mistake by not leaving as he had threatened; therefore, his answer to Mathilde's second letter announces, in effect, that this time he will leave. The result in this comedy of errors is that Mathilde gives him a rendezvous. Without really being conscious of it, Julien has successfully used, on two occasions, a threat of departure to bring about the seduction of Mathilde. He is re-enacting his experience with Mme. de Rênal.

In the interior monolog preceding the rendezvous, Julien sees himself as most assuredly a victim of his imagined conspirators. The scene is perhaps the most exemplary in the novel of the almost paranoic state into which the hero is capable of working himself. It is hardly a question of withdrawing, at this point. Things have progressed too far, and honor forbids him from shirking his duty. A bust of Richelieu silently reproaches him and rids him early of any doubt but that the rendezvous will take place. What he debates is how to rehabilitate his personal honor, how to justify himself after the scandal, the eruption of which looms as a certainty.

That nothing could convince him of the contrary is evidenced by the fact that he "sees" conspiracy in the servants' faces and a medieval grandeur in the face of Mathilde. He is imposing his own fears on reality.

Note how even this impending doom for himself that he sees on Mathilde's face is intimately related with his love for her. "He nearly fell in love with her." The Stendhalian hero permits himself to be afraid without shame, because he has resolved to have the courage before the event itself. This attests to the self-imposed honesty and astringent morality by which Julien lives. He is presented truly as the military commander surveying the battlefield, anxiously awaiting the offensive.

Julien is capable of detachment and of a sort of ironic self-scrutiny. This is a kind of insurance against ridicule that Stendhal permits Julien to create. After all, Julien does not take himself too seriously, just as Stendhal has not been his own dupe.

Julien repents for having sent the letters to Fouqué. He sees the possible circulation of the documents as a base action on his own part, since posterity would see in him an ingrate who would resort to attacking a woman's honor. He is now at the point of preferring to be a dupe, his personal honor requiring self-immolation in silence. Note the rapidity of Stendhal's pace in narration, imitating, thereby, the mental processes of Julien.

Chapter 16 begins without a break from the end of the preceding by the running interior monolog of the hero. Although Julien has never been so afraid in his life, waiting at any moment for the conspirators to strike, he assures himself that he has left no eventuality without consideration, so that he will not be able to reproach himself in the event of a blunder. Arriving at Mathilde's window with his pistol in hand, Julien goes to battle.

The rendezvous scene is rightly reputed as one of Stendhal's masterpieces in psychological analysis. The scene is very dramatic and fast moving. These effects are achieved by the use of short, terse sentences, both by Stendhal in commenting and by the characters in dialog. A second contributing factor is the structure: Stendhal alternates consistently in his presentation first, of Julien's, then of Mathilde's view of the situation, adding commentaries and making analysis after the remarks of each character.

Alternation is necessitated by the nature of the characters and of their love. Both have conceived a role that they are playing, and the roles prove inadequate to the occasion. Such a rendezvous demands passion, spontaneity, forgetfulness of self. Both are self-conscious, scheming, suspicious, acting out a preconceived conduct. It is the bifurcation of two characters into an identical role and their own individual "doubling" in the presence of the other that make the scene basically comic-heroic.

A rapid sketch of their respective states—internal and the manner in which they find external expression—follows: Mathilde has been observing Julien for an hour and is now very emotional. Nonetheless, she addresses him as "Monsieur." Julien has thought only of the ambush he expects, therefore, he is ill-prepared. He remembers, in his embarrassment, that his role requires that he be romantic; therefore, he attempts to embrace Mathilde. Her refusal, stemming, no doubt, from timidity and from her preference of the ideal to the real, puts Julien back on the defensive. This explains his reaction: ". . . overjoyed at being repulsed, he hastened to look around."

Mathilde is delighted to find a topic of conversation, she is so unprepared for this "real" situation. She asks what Julien has in his pockets. Julien, likewise embarrassed, is pleased to have conversational subject matter and explains that he is carrying an "arsenal." Then it is a question of how to dispose of the ladder. Mathilde adopts a tone of normal conversation, admonishing Julien not to break the windows, lamenting over the flowers crushed as the ladder falls.

Julien, seemingly dedicated to the idea of self-defeat, sees Mathilde's supply of rope as proof that Croisenois has triumphed over him after all, since he, Julien, must not be the first to have visited her room. Julien becomes suspicious again, but he has enough resourcefulness and presence of mind to playfully adopt a Creole accent. This effort does not escape Mathilde's attention, and she joins in the game, seeing this as a manifestation of Julien's superiority, thus justifying, in her own eyes, her love for him.

When she takes his arm, his violent reaction is one of suspicion again, and he draws his dagger. There reigns a complicity of silence, as they are listening for a menacing noise. Then returns the embarrassing silence. Julien busies himself with measures of security; Mathilde has just awakened to the compromising situation her daring has put her into. This leads her to ask what has happened to her letters.

Julien, still distrustful, explains the measures he has taken to safeguard himself, believing that his hidden enemies will hear his words. Mathilde's amazement calls forth a sincere avowal on Julien's part of his suspicions. Mathilde has now switched to "tu," but her tone belies this familiarity. This encourages Julien to embrace her, and she only half repulses the embrace.

Now Julien is more the master of himself and, relying on recollection of his past successes, begins reciting love passages from Rousseau. Mathilde, not even hearing them, but carrying on her own mental debate, announces that she finds his courage in coming proof that he merits her love.

Each is attempting to capture reflections of the "self," not to direct attention to the "other." Therefore, what is actually occurring are two separate monologs: Mathilde looking for evidence that Julien is worthy of the sacrifice she has made; Julien looking for encouragement, which in turn will bolster his self-esteem and courage. Stendhal is showing vanity, an early stage of love.

Sensing the emptiness of the familiar address, Julien falls back on his reason, and he is content, momentarily, to found his happiness simply on being preferred by this haughty aristocrat. Now he is searching for a plan of conduct, making conversation to fill the silence; Mathilde joins in this "substitute" action, covering her horror at her own indiscretion by prattle about when they can meet again.

In narrating their conversation, Stendhal has recourse to a method of narration called later "style indirect libre," the initiation of which is attributed to Flaubert. It consists of quoting the words of the characters out of quotes, of narrating as if the characters were speaking. Julien offers his plan, not directly quoted as dialog, but as part of the narration: "What could be easier for them than to meet in the library and make arrangement for everything?" and again: "If Mathilde thought it better for him always to come by means of a ladder, he would expose himself to that slight danger with a heart overflowing with joy. . . ."

Instead of helping to create an air of complicity, thus furthering their rendezvous and speeding it on to its climax, Julien's brilliance and self-assurance awaken Mathilde's pride and make her ask herself again whether Julien is now her master. "If she had been able, she would have annihiliated herself and Julien," says Stendhal, in an abrupt manner, startling the reader. Stendhal prefers classical litotes to romantic hyperbole.

Mathilde had not predicted this attitude of hers; thus do Stendhal's characters watch themselves develop, surprised at what they become. Eventually, her will silences her remorse, timidity, shyness, and wounded modesty, and she notes that she is not fulfilling her role: one speaks to one's lover. She therefore speaks tender words in a cold tone. She forces herself to permit herself to be seduced. From this act, typically hardly alluded to because of Stendhal's great modesty, neither feels pleasure.

Their reactions are different, yet consistent with their character: Julien feels happiness only in retrospect as he rides in "high solitude"; Mathilde wonders why there has been such a distance between her ideal and the real, and she asks whether she really loves Julien. The reaction of both characters echoes Stendhal's own, at his persistent disappointment with reality: N'est-ce que ça? (Is that all it is?) Mathilde has emptied the act of pleasure for Julien because she has undertaken it as a duty to him and to herself. Julien had felt the same reaction after his first rendezvous with Mme. de Rênal. He notices again, however, how inferior is this happiness with Mathilde to that which he knew with Mme. de Rênal.

CHAPTERS 17-20

Summary

In the days following the rendezvous, Mathilde is distant and cold toward Julien. He is perplexed and discovers that he is hopelessly in love with her. Confronting her one day in the library, Julien asks directly if she does not love him any more. Mathilde answers that she is horrified at having given herself to the first one to come along. Julien's reaction is spontaneous: he rushes upon a medieval sword hanging in the room, and after unsheathing it, stops, checks his impulse to kill Mathilde, examines the blade curiously and puts it back. Mathilde sees in the act a truly heroic gesture, worthy of her ancestors. In desperation, Julien announces to the marquis that he is going on a business trip to Languedoc. The marquis has other plans for Julien, who is confined to his quarters to be available at any time for an important mission.

Mathilde now considers Julien worthy of being her master and for a week permits him to walk with her in the garden, while she passionately talks of the love she felt in the past for his rivals. This is torture for Julien, who is suffering all the pangs of jealousy and unhappiness, thinking himself not loved. Blurting out his love for her, Julien finds himself hated again. The course of events increasingly depends upon Julien's imminent departure on the marquis' mission.

By a happy accident, Julien and Mathilde come quite independently to a state of mind propitious to a second midnight rendezvous. Mathilde begins to reproach herself for having been so unkind, then is carried away by the mood and sentiment that an opera inspires in her. Julien, for his part, is in the depths of despair and contemplates suicide as he daringly puts up the ladder and presents himself uninvited at Mathilde's window. Their second rendezvous is less studied and more successful than the previous one. Soon thereafter, however, Mathilde regrets having succumbed and

having shorn her locks and presented them to Julien in a submissive
gesture. Julien has again known, but lost, happiness.

At dinner, Julien finds that he has lost favor at court. He rides all day
in an effort to numb his mind through physical exhaustion. As she confronts
him one morning in the library, Mathilde tells him pitilessly that she does
not love him. She overwhelms him with her vehemence. Julien accidentally
breaks an antique Japanese vase, and his apology to Mme. de la Mole,
made in the presence of Mathilde, intimates that his love, like the vase,
has been irreparably shattered.

Commentary

This four-chapter episode might well have been subtitled their war in
love. Viewed as a whole, it consists of the ups and downs of the stormy
relationship between Julien and Mathilde. Their love undergoes a reversal
from the previous stage. Here, Julien falls madly in love with Mathilde
because of her continued coldness and unavailability. He undergoes all the
anguish, uncertainty, and torment that Mme. de Rênal felt in his affair
with her. Julien has lost his advantage; his triumph has turned to ashes.

Several explanations are possible. Both egotists, the two are so
similar in nature that they are bound to experience love unsuccessfully.
Then, too, this is how love develops, according to Stendhal: it is an
autonomous emotion that reserves unexpected developments for us. It dies,
is revived, overpowers the victim. It is true that in this couple Stendhal
has chosen extreme examples for the demonstration of love.

Mathilde, previously so ardent and the initiator of the rendezvous,
flees Julien, insults and humiliates him. She denies even that she loves
him. Paradoxical in nature, their love resembles that between Rodrique
and Chimène in Corneille's Cid: at moments when they are farthest apart
and when their love seems impossible, they love each other most, since
it is during these moments that they are the most worthy of each other.
Again, Stendhal reminds us that happiness is the energy expended in the
pursuit of happiness.

Unwittingly, Julien has magically dispelled the idealization that
constituted Mathilde's love for him. Since Mathilde has ceased to feel
boredom for the last few months, Stendhal explains, she forgets what it
was like and is now bored by Julien. Mathilde exists only for "magic
moments" of paroxysm when she is placing her entire existence at stake.
Once happiness is realized, it ceases to be interesting. In such a proud soul
as Mathilde, the idea that another would be her master is unbearable. This
fear of domination is another reason for Mathilde's rejection of Julien.

The sword incident demonstrates the paradoxical nature of their
relationship: Mathilde scorns Julien and insults his honor. Julien

reaches blindly for the sword to do her harm, so great is his anger. From this act of malicious intent results a temporary advantage in Mathilde's estimation of Julien, thus in her love for him. She is able to relegate this scene to the medieval past that is the basis of her idealization of their love. She is overjoyed at being on the verge of being killed by her lover. Hurriedly, however, she flees after having recaptured her vision, lest Julien destroy it. Note that the entire dramatic effect of the scene depends upon the image of the sword, chosen with care by Stendhal to jolt the reader.

No novelist succeeds as well as Stendhal in forcing the reader's complicity, unless it be the "new novelists" of contemporary France who are writing what some critics call the "do-it-yourself-novel." In effect, appreciation of Stendhal depends upon the active participation of the reader, who must himself supply the motivation for the acts that Stendhal has his characters commit. The resulting complicity between Stendhal and the reader is particularly operative in episodes such as the love duel between Julien and Mathilde.

Her ideal partially salvaged, Mathilde now readmits Julien to her presence for walks in the garden, where she sadistically forces Julien to listen to her passionate narration of feelings she has felt for his rivals. Mathilde must keep the upper hand, with herself as master and Julien as victim. Only by seeing herself as the master is she able to permit herself to love him. Julien's admission of love to her is a blunder on his part. Sure that he loves her, Mathilde utterly despises him. Mathilde resorts instinctively to these stratagems to keep her love alive in its ideal state. She half hopes that Julien doesn't love her any more, since that would furnish her with a new adventure, permitting her to experience new emotions. The two characters seem to be looking for a safe way to love themselves through the eyes of the other.

Julien has never known such unhappiness. The jealousy that he feels is reminiscent of that felt by Mme. de Rênal. And just as the latter felt pleasure pleading the cause of her rival's, the servant girl's, love for Julien, the hero now praises his rivals in order to "share" the love he thinks Mathilde feels for them.

Stendhal is preparing for Julien's departure, which will occur at the end of Chapter 20, the lowest point and end of Julien's subordinate role in their hateful love. Mathilde projects the future of their relationship, trying to see it as a glorious one, worthy of the ancestry she reveres.

Chapter 19 portrays another partially gratuitous victory for Julien. The thought of suicide inspires him with a courageous act. He will visit Mathilde's room again, then kill himself after she has rebuffed him.

Mathilde might well have rebuffed him, had she not been once again at the "high point" of the idealization cycle.

Mathilde arrives at this point of intoxication in three ways: she continues to project a glorious future for Julien in which she will play a part, then reproaches herself for having acted so cruelly toward him. Second, her idle daydreaming prompts her unconsciously to draw a sketch of Julien. Such an imaginative and romantic nature as Mathilde's could only see this as an almost supernatural sign and proof of her love. The third event congenial to the creation of a receptive frame of mind is the opera that she attends, where again she is able to participate safely, at a distance, idealizing her own love by seeing it in the opera. Stendhal himself sees Mathilde's love as intellectual and contrasts it unfavorably with that felt by Mme de Rênal. The latter's love comes from the heart and does not need to see itself, to examine itself.

Stendhal's intervention to justify Mathilde's character represents an ironic way of condemning those who would condemn his portrait of the times. Mathilde's adventurous and fanciful flights are certainly not to be found in the conduct of the young ladies of his age, he continues, since nineteenth-century France is incapable of great passion. Then, in an apparent contradiction, he introduces his definition of the novel as a mirror carried along a highway. Should it reflect the mire it encounters, the novelist is not to blame, but the mire. Balzac, Stendhal's great contemporary, defends his realism on similar grounds, as had the eighteenth-century French realistic novelists. The point is that even though Mathilde cerebrates her passion, she is capable of one. She, like Stendhal, scorns the apathy and sterility of society.

Discreetly, Stendhal hardly alludes to the rendezvous. By chance, the lovers' exalted moments coincide, and Julien knows happiness reminiscent of that with Mme. de Rênal. The unsolicited avowal of servitude made by Mathilde, betraying her chief concern, Julien will find almost immediately afterward disavowed by her. After having almost half shorn her head and thrown him the locks in a romantic gesture symbolic of her submission, Mathilde, by the next evening, regrets her conduct. She is again at another low ebb in her love, having found only banal reality, much to the bewilderment of Julien.

Chapter 20 confirms the view that Mathilde is playing a game with herself, and Julien is but an instrument. She congratulates herself on the power of her will, which has dominated her love and which has finally permitted her to announce to Julien that she was only deluded into believing that she loved him. Although a conflict is waged in Mathilde's mind between her love and her pride and modesty, she does not appear to be a real victim of love at this stage in their relationship.

Julien's symbolic remark about the vase represents another accidental, clever move. He regrets later having claimed that he no longer loves her, but the avowal, no matter how feigned and insincere, is actually the type of strategy needed to revive Mathilde's love for him.

CHAPTERS 21-23

Summary

The marquis prepares Julien for his role as scribe and spy. Julien will accompany the marquis to a meeting of a group of ultras, where he will take notes on the conversation, condense them with the help of the marquis, memorize the contents, and, inconspicuously dressed, start out on a mission to London. On the way to the meeting, Julien recites a page from the newspaper to the marquis to demonstrate his photographic memory. At the place of rendezvous, the room gradually fills with the plotters. Julien sharpens numerous quills waiting for further orders.

The marquis introduces Julien to the conspirators, and Julien demonstrates to them his prodigious memory. The twelve conspirators would plot means of strengthening the ultras' position against the ever-increasing threat of liberalism, or, as it was termed, jacobinism. The question is whether to ask England to intervene in order to strengthen the ultra monarchy. The marquis is of the opinion that England will help only if the French help themselves by galvanizing their ultra supporters at every level of society. He would recommend severe curtailment of the liberty of the press in an effort to control public opinion.

A cardinal supports the proposal of the marquis, adding the necessity of relying on the power of the Church, whose 50,000 priests have the ear of the people. He suggests that the cabinet minister, M. de Nerval, resign, since he is compromising their cause. Nerval, present among the conspirators, presents himself as favoring the ultra cause against the liberal monarchy. The discussion becomes heated and lasts until three in the morning. The minister leaves, then the Bonapartist, and the remaining conspirators conjecture that the Bonapartist might betray them in an attempt to ingratiate himself with the minister.

Later, Julien and the marquis edit the notes, which Julien memorizes, and the next morning Julien departs on his mission. Stopping at an inn near Metz, Julien encounters the Italian singer Géronimo, who informs Julien that their innkeeper has detained them in order to find a spy who must be apprehended. Julien awakens to find the Jesuit leader of the Besançon Congrégation searching his effects. It is Géronimo who is suspected of being the spy. The singer has been drugged, having fallen into the trap that Julien has avoided.

60

Arriving in London, Julien finally succeeds in meeting the Duke of Wellington, to whom he recites the message in the secrecy of a shabby inn. Julien follows the duke's instructions to go to Strasbourg, then return within twelve days. Julien arrives in Strasbourg, eluding the watchful Jesuits.

Commentary

The mission to which Stendhal has previously alluded is conveniently introduced to create suspense, of course, but also to separate the lovers in order to reverse their roles. Upon his return, Julien will take the offensive. The transition between what preceded and the spy episode was constituted by Mathilde's musings on Julien's future.

Julien has definitely replaced Norbert as a son worthy of the Marquis de la Mole, and for the first time, the marquis explicitly states this preference. Freudians would see in this a disavowal by Stendhal of his own father and a legitimization of his view of himself as one of the "happy few."

Julien gains admittance to the inner sanctum of reactionary power, but he is still an outsider, a role to which he is condemned. He is made painfully aware of this role of outsider-inside by his isolation, obvious only to himself, before the meeting begins. His embarrassment, which he aggravates by endlessly sharpening quills, aptly characterizes Julien as a very self-conscious being. The presence of the Bishop of Agde serves to remind the reader again of the distance covered by our hero, since Julien was also in the role of messenger when the bishop appeared in Verrières.

The affair of the secret note affords another insight into the manner in which Stendhal utilizes actual happenings as a basis for fiction. Although the novel is set in 1830, at the end of the autocratic reign of Charles X, this episode is based upon incidents that took place during the reign of Louis XVIII (1815-24), the more liberal brother of Charles. The memory of Napoleon's One Hundred Days in 1815 and Louis' liberalism actually caused the ultras to plot with foreign powers in an effort to re-establish the reactionary spirit of the "ancien régime." Stendhal's conspirators are speaking "historically," without naming him, of Louis XVIII, although they are "living" under the reign of Louis' successor, Charles X. The "Ordonnances de Juillet" by which Charles X attempted to revoke the Charter embodying the principles of the Revolution of '89 and to stifle freedom of the press precipitated the July Revolution of 1830, which hailed the "bourgeois king," Louis-Philippe, who re-established liberalism and reigned until 1848.

This incident and others of political inspiration in the novel were added by Stendhal after the July Revolution. He could hardly have included them with impunity before that date.

Stendhal has a predilection for the mystery of clandestine operations, of spy intrigue, including secret rendezvous to which only the initiated are admitted. It is at once related to his own adventures (he was pursued by the Austrian police for his liberal views) and simply an indication of the exclusiveness of the "happy few," the elite of whom Stendhal counted himself as one.

Although Julien has definite republican sympathies, he is in the service of legitimists. Aside from aptly describing this social pariah — the idealist who champions the revolutionary cause but who traffics with the enemy out of necessity — Julien's paradoxical position betrays the political ambiguities of Stendhal himself. Defender of liberalism and, at the same time, aspiring to the good old days of the monarchy, Stendhal nonetheless abhorred the idea of a democracy.

Stendhal's apology for inclusion of the political discussion should not be taken too seriously by the reader. Furthermore, the political and social substrata of the novel are the context in which Julien's individual adventure is realized. This is the most illustrious role that Julien will play as an individual subservient to others. His next brief "position" will seem to grant him a momentary social independence. The power hierarchy, so ubiquitous in the novel, is apparent even in this assemblage of the summit. Some are deferential to others, some can be outspoken and ironic, others must be silent.

It should be noted that Stendhal limits the narration strictly to Julien's perception and comprehension of the mysterious proceedings. The reader has the impression that he, too, is an outsider privileged to eavesdrop. We are rarely told any more than Julien knows. When Julien is excluded briefly during the course of the meeting, the reader is also excluded. And we take our cues from Julien, who takes his from interpreting the facial expressions and tone of voice of the Marquis de la Mole.

Three minor characters have reappeared in these chapters: Castanède, Agde, Géronimo. Their reappearance reminds us of Julien's progress: he is now the very successful protégé of the Marquis de la Mole, and he fulfills his mission without a hitch.

CHAPTERS 24-28

Summary

Smitten by love, Julien is unable to amuse himself in Strasbourg. He encounters his London friend, the Russian Prince Korasov, who befriends and undertakes to cheer him. The prince advises Julien how to proceed in his love affair with Mathilde. He must resort to inspiring jealousy in the woman he loves by courting another. The prince gives Julien a series of love letters with directions as to how and when they are to be delivered to the lady. Julien intends to court Mme. de Fervaques, a beautiful widow of a marshal of bourgeois lineage, a prude who is influential in the Congrégation. Julien agrees to the stratagem. At the same time, he turns down an offer made by Korasov for the hand of the latter's cousin, a match that would facilitate a glorious military career for Julien in Russia.

Upon returning to Paris, Julien asks advice of Altamira in his courting of Mme. de Fervaques. Altamira introduces him to Don Diego Bustos, who had unsuccessfully attempted to court this lady. From Bustos, Julien learns how to go about the conquest. At the Moles', Julien must exert much self-control to begin his campaign. Civil but not attentive to Mathilde, he seeks out Mme. de Fervaques and spends the evening in conversation with her. At the theater, his eyes remain fixed on Mme. de Fervaques. Upon seeing Julien again, Mathilde, who has sworn to forget him, to return to virtue, and to hasten her marriage to Croisenois, now reverses her position, seeing in Julien her real husband.

Mathilde is consternated by Julien's indifference for her. Mme. de la Mole now looks upon Julien more favorably, since he seems to be interested in Mme. de Fervaques. Julien copies the first letter and delivers it, following the directions of the prince. During his evening conversations, Julien places himself in such a way that he can observe Mathilde without being seen. Mme. de Fervaques is quite favorably impressed with Julien, in whose eloquence, metaphysical bent, and mystical preoccupation she thinks she sees the making of a great churchman.

Two weeks and many letters later, Julien receives an invitation to dinner at the home of Mme. de Fervaques. Julien finds the dinner, the conversation, and the guests insipid. Tanbeau, his rival at the Hôtel de la Mole, encourages him in his conquest of Mme. de Fervaques.

One evening at the opera, Mme. de Fervaques intimates that whoever loves her must not love Napoleon. Julien interprets this as an avowal of a certain success in his campaign. Julien's carelessness in copying a letter almost causes Mme. de Fervaques to doubt his sincerity, but he succeeds in excusing the blunder. Mathilde is succumbing to his strategy. She admires his machiavellianism in telling Mme. de Fervaques things he obviously does not believe. Mathilde's marriage with Croisenois is imminent, and Julien thinks again of suicide.

Commentary

These chapters relate the next stage in the love of Julien and Mathilde, in which Julien initiates action and painfully gains an ascendancy over Mathilde.

In the form of Korasov, another father-image reappears to take Julien in hand and teach him the art of seduction. Korasov sees Julien's problem immediately. It will be necessary to attract Mathilde's attention to himself away from herself. Julien must make Mathilde see him not as an ideal she has created, but as he is. Korasov's offer to Julien should remind the reader of a similar one made by Fouqué in Part I. The identity of circumstances points up Julien's contrasting situations: in Verrières he refused happiness because he was goaded by ambition; here, he refuses to satisfy that ambition, now silenced by a love of which he is the victim.

Julien is so much the victim of his love that he adopts the point of view of the woman who scorns him to deprecate himself pitilessly. This period of depression that Julien is experiencing Stendhal had analyzed in his treatise on love. Julien sees himself as the most abject of beings, as inferior to Korasov, and at fault for not being loved by the perfect Mathilde.

It is not by chance that Julien chooses Mme. de Fervaques as his instrument. He admits that her beautiful eyes remind him of those loving and passionate eyes of Mme. de Rênal. He longs unconsciously for that experience where he was loved.

Two more mentors are introduced to guide Julien. Altamira and Bustos provide Julien with the necessary information for a seduction. Note that Julien is hypocritical even with his friend Altamira, who is not advised of Julien's stratagem. Stendhal doubtless delights in the dissection of the prude. It is reminiscent of the seduction undertaken in Laclos' *Liaisons Dangereuses* by Valmont of his prudish victim, more sincere, however, in her religious principles than is Mme. de Fervaques. Stendhal's portrayal of the latter as somewhat of an imposter absolves Julien of any guilt, since she is not truly a victim.

The abrupt images betraying Julien's extreme sensibility are meant to convince the reader of the hero's great effort in playing his role. Julien is moved by the sight of the sofa and ladder in the true romantic tradition. Note, however, that the rapid narration and abrupt sentences betoken restraint and a refusal on the part of Stendhal to fall into the raptures and effusiveness of the hyperbole à la Chateaubriand. Julien remains the passive actor of the role carefully outlined by Korasov, acting as a sort of robot. Another note is inserted by Stendhal to show to what extent Julien's ambition is dead. The possibility that the marquis might be named as a minister would give Julien an opportunity to become a bishop. Such a possibility is very far from Julien's present aspiration.

Julien's return has sufficed to change the impetuous Mathilde's plans completely. Mathilde has rationalized her interpretation of virtue to justify her reversal in position. She had decided to return to virtue, but now virtue means legitimizing her love for Julien through marriage: "He's my real husband," blurts out Mathilde.

Note Stendhal's "peeping Tom" tendency (which he has in common with Balzac). The privilege of the superior soul is that he may observe others observing him without their knowledge. Julien is protected by hat brims, his own and that of Mme. de Fervaques, as he observed Mathilde watching him.

Although his love at first incapacitates him for creative action, Julien nonetheless makes progress as an actor and conversationalist. Again, Stendhal states this fact, without offering a demonstration of it. Profiting from his knowledge of Mathilde's character, Julien decides that she will admire him for uttering absurdities with eloquence.

The dinner at the home of Mme. de Fervaques is similar to the one Julien attended in Part I, at the Valenods'. Both present Julien appearing in the enemy camp, and his refusal to take a stand politically is thereby underlined. In Verrières, Julien frequented the society of both liberal and monarchists; here, in spite of his Jansenistic mentor, Pirard, Julien is frequenting the Jesuit milieu. Julien experiences the same feeling of superiority at the two dinners. He had scorned the materialism and bad taste of the Valenods; here, he is disgusted by the pompousness of the guests and by the sterility of the conversation.

Stendhal again underlines Julien's lack of ambition by intimating how he could, were he so inclined, profit from his relationship with Mme. de Fervaques to have himself named a bishop. One aspect of the tragedy of Julien Sorel begins to become apparent. Ironically, he abandoned the tender love of Mme. de Rênal because of his insatiable ambition. He is now reaping the fruits of this ambition—or he could, but he no longer hears that voice—in favor of a love inferior to the one he abandoned.

There is another advantage to feigning a courtship, other than the obvious purpose, which is to inspire jealousy in the real love object. If the victim responds, one may observe the mechanism of love and its progress objectively and with a cool head, hardly possible if one is really in love. Stendhal's own ambition was to achieve an impossible synthesis: to love passionately but without the enslavement of his will and mind.

Mathilde is being taken in by Julien's stratagem, in a different way than he had anticipated, however. She admires his duplicity as she observes him courting Mme. de Fervaques. This means simply that she sees through the stratagem, but that it is nonetheless successful because she is able to relegate this newly discovered quality of Julien to her idealization of him.

Julien's despair reaches its greatest intensity as he again contemplates suicide. Even if he succeeds in reviving Mathilde's love, he knows that it will not produce a lasting effect. He concludes by condemning himself: Why am I myself?

CHAPTERS 29-32

Summary

Mme. de Fervaques is beginning to respond and finally answers Julien's letters. Ultimately, she is writing him a letter daily, which Julien doesn't open and answers with the letters from Korasov. Mathilde, finding the present state of affairs unbearable, encounters Julien one day in the library. She reproaches him from having neglected her, his wife, then collapses in tears. Julien initiates no action in the way of response. Mathilde then reproaches herself for having forgotten her pride, and finding Mme. de Fervaques' letters to Julien all unopened, she is beside herself with rage, insults him, then confessing her love, begs for mercy and faints at his feet. Julien has triumphed.

Mathilde asks Julien if Mme. de Fervaques has shown him proof of her love. Julien answers no, indirectly and diplomatically. He demands guarantees from Mathilde that she will not continue this cruel game with him. She has nothing but the "intensity of her love and her unhappiness if he no longer loves her." Julien withdraws respectfully, requesting time to reflect. Mathilde has found happiness in renouncing her pride. Julien feels obligated to appear in Mme. de Fervaques' box at the opera. The latter mistakenly believes that the tears in Julien's eyes are shed for her. Julien catches sight of Mathilde in another box, weeping.

Going to her box, Julien hears Mathilde murmur tearfully "guarantees." Giving himself over to the expansive joy of his love in the solitude of his room, Julien hits upon a new stratagem to perpetuate Mathilde's love: he must frighten her. The next day she offers to elope with him. He rejects the offer, reminding her that this mood would soon pass. Walking in the garden with Mathilde, Julien confesses how he used to watch for her there, but he then denies immediately the truth of this avowal. He continues to write to Mme. de Fervaques, despite Mathilde's disapproval.

Mathilde is now truly in love. She acts recklessly, but Julien maintains caution. She announces triumphantly, to Julien's consternation, that she is pregnant, and that this is the guarantee which he demanded. She insists on informing her father, but defers to Julien's view that it would be better to delay in writing the letter. In her letter, Mathilde assumes all blame and expresses the hope that her father will forgive both of them. She announces her intention of marrying Julien, and she suggests that their future situation will depend upon how M. de la Mole receives this news.

Commentary

These chapters narrate the victory that Julien wins over Mathilde as his stratagem succeeds. It is here that the Cornelian nature of their love is most fully exemplified: they are nearest when farthest apart. Julien can force an avowal from Mathilde only by refusing to respond in any way to her successive anger, tears, scorn, then tenderness. Note that Julien does not utter a word in this interview. He must not betray his extreme joy, and they seem condemned to love each other separately.

This scene in Chapter 29 is the exact antithesis of a normal love scene. Instead of mutual tenderness and intimacy leading to a reciprocal avowal, there is a progression in hostility and silence leading to an avowal of defeat and submission. Mathilde's initial eruption is spontaneous—she reproaches Julien for having neglected her. Her next reaction is equally spontaneous, but results from the first—she has humiliated herself and weeps tears of shame. Julien proves that he has progressed in controlling his sensibility by treating her with impassive coldness. His lack of response intensifies her shame to the point that she explodes in anger. Opening the drawer and finding the letters unopened, Mathilde next resorts, in her uncontrollable rage, to insults. Instantly repenting, however, she avows her love and faints. Julien can only enjoy his love as a triumph when his victim is reduced to unconsciousness, as an object. This scene no doubt inspired Proust in his demonstration of the impossibility of possessing another through love. Stendhal's portrayal of Mathilde in this scene is an excellent example of the author's unique character presentation. The reader seems to witness at first hand a process of becoming that is simultaneous with the character's acts. It has been said that the words as Stendhal uses them do more than they say. Mathilde faints because she is one of those superior beings whose emotional makeup is so intense that beyond a certain point, it shuts out reality. Julien reacted similarly in his initial interview with Pirard.

Note the Mme. de Fervaques remains hypocritical, even toward herself. She does not admit to herself that she is beginning to love Julien, and since her pride would suffer by addressing letters to him, she is reduced to requesting that he give her self-addressed envelopes. There is a faint glimpse of the role played by Mme. de Rênal as confidante to Elise; however, Stendhal chooses not to exploit it. Mme. de Fervaques confides in Mathilde and asks her advice on how to deal with Julien.

Stendhal utilizes chapter division to isolate and put into relief a scene, or part of a scene, as is evidenced by the artificial chapter division between 29 and 30. The latter in fact continues the previous scene, but the dramatic effect inherent in 29 would not have been otherwise achieved. Chapter 30 rounds out Julien's victory. He continues to exert incomparable self-control, to the point of hypocritically telling Mathilde that he loves Mme. de Fervaques. Finally, he comes to the conscious awareness of the necessity of maintaining a distance in order to continue to be loved by Mathilde. The reader has long since been aware of this fact.

The short scene that concludes Chapter 30 represents a different angle of vision from which to see the situation between Julien and Mathilde. They appear at the opera separately, yet in their separateness they are similarly affected. Both are reduced to tears; both are enjoying their love vicariously by association with the spectacle itself. Julien is permitted to maintain the superiority of the unobserved observer.

The glance that the eyes bestow is a means of communication between the elect, believes Stendhal. Thus, he gives much importance to the role of Julien's eyes in his adventures. In 31, Julien hides his eyes as he sits near Mathilde at the opera, lest they betray his true feelings.

Note in Stendhal's intervention to express approval of Julien's progress, the use of the present tense and "may." These are intended to convince the reader of the veracity of the narrative and is a much abused device to which eighteenth- and nineteenth-century novelists resort. The result is the complicity so vehemently denounced by the "new French novelists": the omniscient novelist would pass off fiction as truth; and in this complicity, the public agrees to pretend that what it is reading is indeed fact. It might be argued that Stendhal in particular needs to establish such a complicity, since his practice of withholding proof of his hero's superiority might alienate the reader.

Stendhal prefers the garden as a setting for amorous adventures. Julien's affair with Mme. de Rênal began and progressed in the garden. The garden scene in 31 evokes Julien's solitary anguish as he watched for Mathilde when he thought he wasn't loved. It is also the setting of the reversal of a previous meeting between them: Mathilde tortured Julien to maintain her ascendancy by telling him of her past loves; now, Julien, momentarily giving way to an expression of his "past" love for her, uses the same stratagem to maintain his present supremacy over Mathilde. He brutally denies the veracity of the words he has just spoken. Julien is testing Mathilde to ascertain to what degree his unchecked sincerity has dampened her love. His own "guarantee" consists of continuing to write the letters. He realizes that he must keep Mathilde in constant doubt as to whether he loves her.

Chapter 32 presents at once the culmination of their conflict, the transformation of Mathilde's love, and it puts into motion the subject matter to be fully developed in the next few chapters.

Circumstances somewhat beyond Julien's control seem to give a new direction to their relationship. Things are getting out of hand for Julien. Mathilde has accepted him as her master, it is true. Her proud nature requires that she continue the struggle elsewhere, however. First, by her reckless, almost promiscuous conduct with a social inferior, she flouts respectability. Mathilde's pregnancy is the beginning of the end for Julien. For Mathilde, it is the renewal in a different form of her dream of heroism and martyrdom. Her duty, she informs Julien, is to inform her father of this turn of events, and joyfully, she sees this heroic act as a way of proving her merit in Julien's eyes and as a way to compete with him in bravery.

Julien has succeeded in convincing Mathilde that her love for him is stronger than his for her. This satisfies Mathilde, giving her a kind of superiority over him. The letter to her father, her "best friend," is certainly consistent with Mathilde's character. Love is for her so intimately associated with the infliction of pain on herself and others that she logically turns to the person she loves best after Julien to initiate a new conflict. A "great soul" requires that others of the elect participate in a kind of ritualistic sacrifice. Fabrice in *The Charterhouse of Parma* has a similar demanding relationship with the other elect in that novel.

The next three chapters recount a struggle of wills between Mathilde and M. de la Mole.

CHAPTERS 33-35

Summary

After reading Mathilde's letter, the marquis is beside himself with rage and hurls every insult at Julien. Julien offers to commit suicide or to be killed by the marquis' men. He goes to Pirard for advice. Mathilde learns of Julien's suicide note, resolutely tells her father that if Julien dies, she dies, and that she will appear as Julien's widow to society. When Julien returns to Paris, Mathilde convinces him to leave and to let her manage her father. The latter only shows indecision. Mathilde refuses to negotiate other than on the condition of a marriage with Julien, heedless of what their future might be. In a moment of tenderness, the marquis gives shares worth 10,000 francs to Mathilde for Julien. Julien stays with Pirard, who has become Mathilde's best ally in trying to convince the marquis of the necessity of a public marriage.

The marquis cannot bring himself to act. He alternately envisions Julien's accidental death, then entertains the wise counsel of Pirard. Above all, he refuses to believe that his ambition for Mathilde's brilliant future has been thwarted. Mathilde has been seeing Julien almost daily at Pirard's. Finally, the marquis gives the couple an estate in Languedoc as a means to put off making a final decision. By letter, Mathilde begs her father's permission to marry Julien. This causes the marquis to consider the possibility of protecting Julien, of helping him to build a brilliant career. He has a doubt, however, about Julien's sincerity. Has he merely used Mathilde as a means to get ahead in society? Rather than give his permission for the marriage, he gives Julien a title and a commission in the army. Mathilde replies by trying to bargain. She will not communicate news of the title to Julien, unless her father agrees to the marriage. The marquis refuses categorically, demands that Julien leave for Strasbourg or all will be rescinded.

Julien prepares to leave for Strasbourg. Pirard explains how the marquis has bought Frilair's silence in order to gain acceptance of the fictitious noble ancestry he has devised for Julien. For five days the latter is in Strasbourg, where his calm dignified bearing, elegance, daring, and ability with arms inspire admiration in his men. Then a letter from Mathilde arrives announcing that all is lost and calling for Julien's immediate return to Paris. There Julien learns that the marquis has inquired of Mme. de Rênal about Julien's past. The answer she has written confirms the fears of the marquis. The letter accuses Julien of making a practice of insinuating himself into respectable families, of seducing the womenfolk, then of ruining them. Julien leaves immediately for Verrières, arriving on a Sunday morning. He buys revolvers, goes to the church, and shoots Mme. de Rênal.

Commentary

In a crisis Julien's women are able to act more efficaciously than he is. Mme. de Rênal resolutely initiated the deception of her husband; Mathilde confronts her father successfully. She is more resolute than her father and turns his indecision to her advantage. The passivity that Stendhal bestows on Julien provides the opportunity for enjoyment of maternal affection that the premature death of Stendhal's own mother denied him.

Twice in Chapter 33 Stendhal describes Julien's conduct as tartuffian. As a defense against the marquis' anger, Julien tries to justify his action, all the while expressing his gratitude to the marquis. Then, Julien adopts the required air of contrition to confess his situation to Pirard, in the hope of getting advice. In Julien's initial confrontation with the marquis, the only solution the former can hit upon is suicide, or letting himself be killed, a solution he doubtlessly offers without reflection. The thought of his "son" comes to him for the first time, however, and this thought checks his willingness to be killed. Julien plays an extremely passive role in Chapters 33 and 34.

Chapter 34 narrates the give and take between Mathilde and her father. He sits in irresolution; Mathilde presses him by letter. The marquis grants a concession, and this encourages Mathilde to ask for more. Another concession is forthcoming from her father, rather than a definitive action that would condone their marriage. Although the marquis is more sympathetically treated by Stendhal than was M. de Rênal, both have the same role in the author's playing out of his oedipus complex.

The marquis' doubting of Julien's motivation is a preparation for the event that will bring about the latter's downfall. A parallel development to this preparation, however, is the momentary "taste" of success that Stendhal will allow his hero to have. Stendhal will accord a title and a regiment to Julien. This is typical treatment by Stendhal of his superior beings. They are not destined for a permanent, commonplace happiness, which would, in fact, become vile to them.

Note that Julien already seems far away from the action. His thoughts are absorbed completely by the future of his child. Stendhal begins attenuating Julien's love for Mathilde, and his ambition is reappearing. Stendhal mentions Julien's ambition twice in this chapter. Julien's joy is boundless at the news that he is an officer of the Hussars. He is aware, however, of the ephemeral nature of this goal attained, as he remarks that his story has reached its climax. Julien still misunderstands situations, however, as he attributes his success to himself alone. He has succeeded in making himself loved by this monster of pride. And he summarizes his present situation astutely when he muses that Mathilde cannot live without him, nor M. de la Mole without her.

How many events, and of what moment, Stendhal crowds into Chapter 35. He moves Julien to the pinnacle of success, lets him revel in this glory for the duration of one page, then precipitates events that will divest him of this worldly glory and ultimately destroy him. The marquis has again been Julien's fairy godfather who conjures up the illusion of success and glory, then takes it from him abruptly.

The scene sketched by Stendhal of Julien in all his equestrian glory evokes briefly the same scene in Part I where Julien played a role in the honor guard. The scenes have in common their illusory nature: then, Julien was merely in the costume of a soldier; now, the abrupt ending of the real role makes its very existence seem doubtful.

Proof of the fact that Julien himself almost believes in his fictitious nobility is furnished by the letter he sends to Chélan, together with money to be distributed to the poor. This is the noble gesture of an aristocrat. Julien wants to believe in his nobility, since he would not consider himself a monster if Sorel, a man whom he despises, were not his father. In this way, the tragic contradiction he has been forced to live—a superior soul stifled by mediocrity—would be reconciled.

Happiness; for the superior being, is simply not available except in small, almost unbearable doses. The proximity of Stendhal to his hero is again underlined. Stendhal is self-demanding, almost masochistic, and his hero, to whom he denies happiness, is superior because of the denial.

We have noted that Stendhal has already begun to exclude Julien's intimate reactions. This tendency is even more pronounced in Chapter 35 as Julien returns hurriedly to Paris, learns what the catastrophe is, takes to the road again, arrives in Verrières, arms himself, and shoots Mme. de Rênal. It is partially Stendhal's reserve, his timidity, his refusal to let himself be seen that has dictated his attitude in narrating these events almost devoid of reference to the psychology that prompts Julien to act. This ambiguity has given rise to a literary debate that continues to our day. Is this act, the attempted murder of Mme. de Rênal, consistent with the character of Julien? Is Stendhal betraying that psychology in an effort to remain faithful to the historical episode that inspired the novel, and is the denouement therefore artificial? Here are some of the critics' views.

Emile Faguet, noted nineteenth-century critic, saw Julien as committing a senseless act that contradicts his character as established by Stendhal. Faguet denies Stendhal a great degree of intelligence, moreover. He sees Julien as the ruthless, ambitious man, coldly calculating and of unshakable will. The character thus conceived, continues Faguet, Julien should have realized that within a short time the marquis, already having accepted many compromises, would have reversed his decision and sanctioned the marriage. Julien seems to have forgotten that he is master of the situation. The denouement, concludes Faguet, seems a little more false than is permitted.

A contemporary critic, M. Henri Rambaud, defends Faguet's interpretation, seeing Julien simply as the "arriviste" type. These critics would see, therefore, the rapidity and incomplete nature of the narration of these events as evidence of Stendhal's dilemma, his avowal, by omission, of the contradiction he was creating in Julien's character.

On the other hand, the contemporary critic Henri Martineau sees this act and the dry, sketched narration leading to it as logical, given the character of Julien. Here is the extremely sensitive, impetuous hero who has throughout the novel attempted, with varying degrees of success, to submit his spontaneity to the discipline of self-control, to disguise his true feelings by hypocrisy. Such a type is capable, as his past conduct has shown, of seeing his discipline thwarted by the sudden eruption of his passion. When this occurs, the act is but the next movement from its inspiration. Therefore, Stendhal is obliged to reduce the narration to its barest elements, to get Julien there, to have him commit the act. The narration reflects the motivation: Julien is in a semi-somnambulistic state. He has but one idea — revenge on Mme. de Rênal — and any other detail would be extraneous.

And why does Julien want revenge? Herein lies the psychological insight of Stendhal. Julien both hates and loves Mme. de Rênal. He has never reached the end of his love for her, yet she has apparently deliberately lied about his conduct. She has ruined his success. His pride and sense of honor have also been wounded. He must avenge himself. Julien's sudden awakening after the act, his long sleep in the jail resulting from excessive tension — these, argues Martineau, are proof that Julien has acted consistently with his character.

Note the scene of the attempted murder. Julien is unable, at first, to fire on Mme. de Rênal because he recognizes her. The bell rings at that moment marking the Elevation of the Host. Mme. de Rênal bows her head, and he no longer recognizes her so clearly. He fires. Only when she ceases to exist momentarily, as herself, defined as an individual whom he loves, is he capable of the act. The ringing of the bell might be instrumental also in the very commission of the act. Its abrupt occurrence, followed by another action, the bowing of heads, calls for another: the firing of the pistol. This would constitute a sort of demotivation of the act, reminiscent of Gide's attempts to produce the gratuitous act in *Les Caves du Vatican* and of Camus' scene in *L'Etranger,* where Meursault through the complicity of things — the sun's reflection, heat — fires on the Arab. Here, there is a "chain of events," one producing another, an inexorable rhythm created thereby, to which Julien almost involuntarily and mechanically contributes.

CHAPTERS 36-39

Summary

Julien is imprisoned in Verrières, unaware that Mme. de Rênal has miraculously escaped death and that the kind treatment he receives in prison is due to her intervention. He writes his farewell to Mathilde, requesting that she never attempt to see him again. Julien is overjoyed to learn that Mme. de Rênal is not dead. He has confessed numerous times to the public prosecutor who visits him, and he hopes, by this means, to simplify the procedure and to be left alone. He is moved to another prison in a gothic tower in Besançon. He begins to relive his past with Mme.

de Rênal and finds that there was happiness. He contemplates suicide, then rejects the idea.

Julien receives the visits of Chélan and Fouqué. Chélan disheartens him, weakening his courage. Fouqué cheers him. The interrogations continue, in spite of Julien's frank avowal of guilt. Fouqué attempts to intervene by means of a visit to Frilair. The latter is increasingly intrigued by the mystery of the Sorel affair, and he will attempt to benefit from it. Julien hopes not to have to endure a visit from his father, and Fouqué is horrified at this lack of filial love.

Mathilde visits Julien, disguised as Madame Michelet. She has made overtures everywhere to gain Julien's release. Of these attempts she tells him nothing. Julien finds her extremely attractive, and, out of respect and admiration, he abandons himself with ecstasy to her love. Mathilde has visited Frilair, leader of the Besançon Congrégation, erstwhile enemy of her father. She discloses to Frilair enough information to arrive at a sort of bargain: she will exercise her influence in Paris to Frilair's advantage, in exchange for Frilair's assurance that he will work for the acquittal of Julien.

Mathilde has requested that Mme. de Fervaques use her influence with a bishop to negotiate with Frilair. Mathilde has bribed the guards to gain constant access to Julien. The latter reproaches himself for not appreciating Mathilde's superhuman efforts to save him or her passionate ecstasies. He proposes that she turn over their child to Mme. de Rênal. Mathilde, offended at this suggestion, finds that she is increasingly obliged to fight against Julien's growing inclination for solitude and against an awakening of affection for Mme. de Rênal. He returns to the subject of his child's future, but approaches it more diplomatically.

Commentary

From this point on, Julien's life will be lived in the jail cell. Although his physical life will be severely limited, his mental and psychological life will be very active, and he will ultimately know the happiness he has sought, once the voice of ambition stills itself, out of necessity. Julien will arrive at a sort of self-knowledge. Here begin to unfurl the various preoccupations of Julien that will be fully developed in later chapters: his decreasing interest in Mathilde and the ever-increasing thought of Mme. de Rênal; his meditations on death, courage, and happiness.

Let us analyze one of Julien's states of mind. Finally emerging from his hypnotic state, Julien's first comment is that it is over, there is only death awaiting him, either by the guillotine or by suicide. Then he falls asleep. It is as if he realizes the necessity of steeling himself, of adopting an attitude, in order to avoid falling into the anguish of fear. His defiant confession to the judge is simply a refusal to submit to the humiliation of being judged, reserving this right for himself. Next he feels the tiresome duty of reporting to Mathilde, to inform her of his act of vengeance, to request that she forget him. It is not only an accounting to his partner in heroism to prove that he is worthy, but also the expression of an unconscious wish to be rid of her.

Then comes the first awesome realization of the death that awaits him. At the hint of the appearance of fear, Julien rallies his courage, rejects the idea of remorse by rationalization: he has been wronged; he has wronged: he must be punished. He rounds out this reasoning by scorning society, which might see some glory in his execution only if he were to scatter gold among the people on his way to the scaffold. Stendhal's presentation of Julien as the victim of society, condemned not for the crime of attempted murder but for not accepting his place in that society, no doubt inspired Camus in his portrayal of Meursault in *L'Etranger*. Meursault killed an Arab, but he is found guilty because he did not weep at his mother's funeral. Meursault's acceptance of the verdict echoes many of Julien's thoughts of these final chapters.

Julien's carefully constructed mask is completely destroyed when he learns that Mme. de Rênal is not dead at all. At this news, Julien is reduced instantaneously to a simple, defenseless child in tears, and he sees the will of God in his act. Only now does Julien permit himself to feel repentance for his crime, and it is his own renewed love for Mme. de Rênal that prompts his joyous cry that she will live, then, to love him still. Momentarily, he thinks now of escape, but dismisses the idea, since it would depend upon bribing the ignoble jailor.

Julien's prison tower cell affords him a beautiful view. It is another of the symbols of the elevated isolation of the superior soul. Stendhal puts Fabrice in a similar situation in *The Charterhouse*. Moreover, Fabrice comes to prefer the prison to freedom, since he has fallen in love with the jailor's daughter. It will be only in such solitude, safely shut off from the world, that Julien will find happiness. Note that in Stendhal's view the hero is less excluded from society by his imprisonment than is society denied access to the hero.

Julien resigns himself again, however, to the justice of the death penalty. Life is not boring for him, since he begins to see it from a new slant. Julien is amazed at what is happening to him inwardly. Stendhal's heroes watch themselves, discover themselves. There is nothing predetermined about them, in the sense that characters are often "flat" and never surprise us. Balzac tends to create flat characters; Stendhal's are round, using the terminology of E. M. Forster *(Aspects of the Novel)*. It is this aspect of Stendhal's character portrayal that has found much favor with contemporary existentialistic critics. The Stendhalian hero is forced to be free, is condemned to the eternal state of becoming. He discovers himself daily in order to remake himself.

What are these perceptions of his glorious future in prison? Julien's rediscovery of the happiness he had with Mme. de Rênal and of the fact that he still loves her. Stendhal's analysis of Julien operates by the associational method: remorse makes Julien think of Mme. de Rênal and of his past happiness; at other times, thinking that he might have killed her, Julien swears that, in that event, he would have committed suicide; suicide, an imagined consequence of that past possibility, then looms as a possibility in the present. Still measuring himself against Napoleon, Julien rejects suicide, since Napoleon went on living. The end of Chapter 36 finds Julien temporarily happy with his present surroundings.

Julien's imprisonment will be punctuated by intermittent visitors. Even here he cannot escape the outside world. Note the contrasting effects that his visitors have on him: the aged Chélan presents to Julien only the image of death and decay, in spite of his reasoning that his own death in the prime of life ought to dispel such a vision; the antidote is the vision of the sublime afforded by the simplicity, sincerity, and artless friendship of Fouqué.

Part of Stendhal's uniqueness for his age as a psychological novelist is obscured to us by the developments in the novel posterior to Stendhal, and to which we are very much accustomed. Stendhal was one of the first novelists to portray how the individual is altered by the influence exerted upon him from surrounding reality. In this respect, he antidates naturalism. Such alternations have in fact, been carefully noted throughout the novel be Stendhal, but they are particularly noticeable during the episode relating Julien's imprisonment. Here, any intrusion on Julien's isolation produces dramatic reactions in his soul.

Julien hits upon the idea of the thermometer to measure his courage, and this gives rise to his resolution to be courageous when it will be required of him. We have already witnessed Julien's tendency to bolster his courage in the present by assuring himself of his future self-control.

Although he is safely imprisoned, Julien is still the victim of society and of its intrigues. This theme is taken up again by Stendhal and will be amplified in what follows.

Julien plays almost no role in Chapter 38. More hints are given that he is losing interest in Mathilde. The time has come for Mathilde to play out in reality her ideal dream of heroic self-sacrifice for her own version of Boniface de la Mole. The Julien-Mathilde continues to be Cornelian: Julien now really merits her love, since Mathilde may assume that what prompted his crime was love for her. This incarnation in Julien of her ideal plus his increasing indifference toward her will intensify Mathilde's love. She seems in fact to love Julien desperately, even though Stendhal will tell us that this love needs the third party to witness it. That is, Mathilde's heroic efforts to save Julien at the risk of loss of her own reputation are partially inspired by her need to impress the world, to be admired by others. She aspires to see herself loving Julien as others would see her. Hers is still an intellectual love.

Mathilde's visit to Frilair is reminiscent of Julien's entrance into the seminary. Both must screw up their courage as they approach the lion in his den. The confrontation between Mathilde and Frilair might be considered a battle in ruse in which Mathilde will not have the upper hand. Nevertheless, Frilair and Mathilde are fairly evenly matched as adversaries, and, in the end, both will be duped.

The action in Chapter 39 takes place wholly in Julien's cell. At first there is not one specific incident narrated; rather several visits, all similar, are fused to comprise a typical one in which the attitude of Mathilde and Julien are contrasted. The final conversation closing the short chapter becomes the result of what precedes and stands for one specific visit. Here is represented one of Stendhal's typical methods of narration.

Julien is tired of heroism. He is more virtuous now than at any time in his life, since ambition no longer goads him. Therefore, he reproaches himself for what he has done to the marquis and Mathilde de la Mole. It is here that Stendhal advises us that Julien, unwittingly, is hopelessly in love with Mme. de Rênal. Julien's awareness of this fact is dim, expressing itself only in his desire to give his offspring to Mme. de Rênal. Rebuffed by Mathilde, Julien artfully returns to the same subject, expressed in terms that would appeal to Mathilde's turn of mind. Note that Stendhal does not comment on Julien's stratagem. His conduct toward Mathilde is reminiscent of that which he adopted in his "seduction" of Mme. de Fervaques. This is the first manifestation of Julien's new attitude toward Mathilde. He relies on duplicity to convince her. Later, as he becomes increasingly irked by her presence, he will punish her somewhat sadistically.

Note, in Julien's presentation, Stendhal's own preoccupation with the future. Stendhal was convinced that his real public would be that of the twentieth century. The appearance of the idea of abolishment of capital punishment, a burning issue today, would bear out Stendhal's conviction that he was writing for the future.

Summary

Just before his trial, Julien pleads guilty of premeditated attempted murder to the judge and to his own defense lawyer, who visit his cell. Mathilde has succeeded in establishing a contact between Mme. de Fervaques and M. de Frilair, with the result that promise has been intimated of a bishopric for Frilair in exchange for his willingness to influence the jurors. Frilair is certain of being able to control the votes of Valenod, de Moirod, and of Cholin, and of being able to bring about an acquittal. In spite of the protests of her husband, Mme. de Rênal has come to Besançon and has personally written a plea of mercy for Julien to each of the thirty-six jurors.

All of Besançon has turned out for the trial. Mathilde makes a final tearful visit to Frilair, who assures her that all has been arranged, that the jurors will vote as Valenod votes. Julien has decided not to speak out in his own defense at the trial. The trial begins. The audience, mostly women, is obviously sympathetic toward the defendant. The trial lasts far into the night with no recess. Julien delivers a final oration after the summation, in spite of his resolve not to speak. The jury returns with a verdict of guilty with premeditation. Julien's only comment to the court is that he has been justly condemned to death.

Julien is moved to the death cell. His thoughts are only of Mme. de Rênal, whom he would hope to see before he dies. Mathilde disturbs his peaceful sleep to plead that he appeal for another trial. Julien stands firm in his refusal, in spite of Mathilde's entreaties. Julien gives the same answer to his lawyer, and he feels more kindly disposed toward the lawyer as they depart than he does toward Mathilde.

Commentary

These chapters relate the trial and the events immediately anterior and posterior to it.

Julien's soliloquy reveals his calm acceptance of the inevitability of his death. This attitude is in marked contrast to the frantic activity of Mathilde and Mme. de Rênal to bring about his acquittal. Julien remains ignorant of their attempts, and the ironic result is that they are working at cross purposes: Julien admits premeditation; but Mme. de Rênal urges the jurors not to find premeditation; Julien refuses to consider a plea of jealousy, as Mathilde, swallowing her pride, urges him to plead.

Chapter 40 brings Mme. de Rênal back into focus, in preparation for the final role she will play in the last chapters. The movement of the short chapter shifts from Julien's cell to the final efforts of Mathilde with Frilair, and finally to the passionate plea for mercy that is Mme. de Rênal's letter. In passing, Stendhal alludes to the effect that the trial has had on Besancon. This adds to the brief, but complete and suspenseful, summing up of everyone's pretrial state.

Note the point at which Julien has arrived in his elaboration of an "art of living." In his own mind, his affair is already classified. He is finally enjoying a life in which he may give himself over completely to contemplation, to dreams of past happiness with Mme. de Rênal, to an objective, dispassionate self-scrutiny and evaluation. Any invasion of his privacy by sordid details of life outside his cell is painful to him. Freudians would see in the Stendhalian hero's passive, blissful state achieved in the protectiveness of prison Stendhal's desire to return to the womb. When maternal Mme. de Rênal finally joins Julien in this happy seclusion, such a view is even more convincing.

We witness the trial scene from Julien's point of view. Thus, the reader adopts Julien's physical vantage point, and he observes not individual faces in the courtroom, but groups of faces, mostly feminine, localized only generally by their position vis-à-vis Julien. Across from the dock above the jurors and judge, twelve to fifteen pretty women occupy three galleries. In the circular gallery overhanging the crowded courtroom are more young, pretty faces. Just as he enters the courtroom, Julien glimpses the gothic pillars, an isolated and clear detail of the blurred scene that surrounds him. After his initial view, by means of a wide sweep Julien's attention is attracted to the galleries above the jury, where he sees Mme. Derville. Only once does the point of view stray—to appreciate Julien's simple elegance as viewed by the ladies of the courtroom. The description is incomplete and fragmentary, but in that respect realistic. It is a foretaste of Stendhal's great battle scene in the *Charterhouse* in which the battle of Waterloo is seen from the point of view of an individual soldier, who is never quite sure of what is transpiring. This realistic technique was admired and imitated by the great Tolstoy. *The Red Badge of Courage*, by Stephen Crane, portrays war realistically in much the same way that Stendhal had done.

Is it accurate to say that Julien commits suicide? Again, Stendhal does not offer an explicit answer. The answer lies partially in another question: would Valenod have betrayed Julien had the latter not denounced the society that condemns him? Stendhal has been careful to reintroduce Valenod intermittently and to assert Valenod's jealousy of Julien, who had succeeded in making Mme. de Rênal his mistress. Would this hatred and desire for vengeance have sufficed to cause Valenod to instruct the jury to condemn Julien, or was Julien's brutal condemnation of the aspiring bourgeoisie the final blow that precipitated the betrayal?

At any rate, it is because of his accurate evaluation of the situation, and because of his courage in proclaiming it to others, that Julien plays a truly heroic role in the court scene. Julien tells the jury that he will be condemned not for having committed the crime, but for having violated the social hierarchy, for having risen above his class. Julien, like Camus' Meursault, executes a reversal in position: the accused condemns the accuser. In a sense, Julien assumes the way in which he will die: he rejects the death penalty unless he, first, has admitted its justice. In this regard, he is the ancestor of Malraux's heroes, who do not undergo death passively, but who assume their death.

To what extent is Julien aware of the gravity of the consequences of his oration, assuming that it did incite Valenod to betrayal? It would not appear to have been a deliberate attempt to bring about his own condemnation, rather it is prompted by his sense of duty, which arises spontaneously. His manner during the trial is one of dignity and courage, although he has difficulty at times in controlling his emotions. During his emotional moments, Julien is seeing himself as the lady spectators see him. The oration would simply be another of those moments when Julien's sensibility betrays him. An impulsive awakening of emotion catches his mask of self-control and calm off guard. That Julien is aware of how others are viewing him during this trial when his life is in the balance should not surprise us too much. This is another faithful rendition of psychological truth by Stendhal. In crucial moments, immediate reactions will many times be quite far from the vital issue. Julien seems to view his trial with a certain objectivity.

One critical view holds that Julien unconsciously harbors a death wish. Such a view would give more responsibility to Julien in the resulting verdict of guilty.

Another view would see in Julien simply another example of the fate of the Stendhalian creature who, having lived so intensely, has burned himself out. It would be the extension on a grander scale of such phenomena as Mathilde's involuntary fainting, of Julien's loss of consciousness in the presence of Pirard, of La Sanseverina's falling asleep while seated in the *Charterhouse*. Such an interpretation of Julien's role in his own condemnation would be in keeping with Stendhal's romantic conception of character.

Even after the death sentence is read, Julien keeps his aplomb and inner calm. He lucidly examines the act of vengeance that Valenod has committed and muses momentarily on what will await him after life. Recalled to reality by Mathilde's cry, Julien's thoughts come with haste and confusion, but he contains these and expresses outwardly only his approval of the death penalty.

Note that the most strained emotional moments undergone by the characters are related with the most clipped, terse, and abrupt prose by Stendhal.

Stendhal continues to "detach" Julien from the action, a tendency we first noticed when the hero left to assume his commission in the army. Now that he is condemned to death, Julien's detachment is even more strongly pronounced. In musing about himself, Julien utilizes the past tense. He sees himself as having already been guillotined, which produces the effect of an even greater degree of objectivity achieved by Julien. This approach and the ironic self-detachment characterizing his interior monolog are no doubt a sort of defense mechanism. Julien is steeling himself in order not to give way to the horror of death. At the same time, it is part of the new happiness, the "art of living" that Julien has perfected now that he is in the seclusion of the prison cell.

Unconsciously, Julien is punishing Mathilde for all the humiliations she has imposed on him, as he refuses to give serious thought to her appeals. He even solicits her praise at his courtroom heroism, which is reminiscent of the ideal that characterized their love. In a sense, Julien has been victorious in their heroic rivalry: he has invited death and refused to appeal the sentence. It is quite possible that Mathilde feels somewhat cheated. Julien is destroying her own heroic role.

Stendhal depicts for us here a truly superior soul. Julien is moved by genuine suffering, sensitive, but proud to the point of refusing to expose his suffering to the view of others, thus to debasement. The tiresome presence of Mathilde succeeds only intermittently in piercing the reverie that increasingly characterizes the mental life of Julien. He imagines Mme. de Rênal's reaction after his death. Stendhal is preparing for the long-awaited arrival of Julien's first and only love.

CHAPTERS 43-45

Summary

Julien is overjoyed by a visit from Mme. de Rênal. He agrees to appeal if she will visit him every day in his cell. They know complete happiness. After three days, M. de Rênal has ordered that his wife return to Verrières. An ambitious priest has undertaken the conversion of Julien and has posted himself in all weather outside the prison, where much to Julien's annoyance, he attracts a great crowd. In desperation, Julien admits him, then rids himself of the troublesome priest by sending him to say masses for the poor.

Mathilde arrives on the heels of the departing priest to relate the treachery of Valenod and to try to convince Julien of the necessity of requesting a reprieve. Julien finally sends her away, requesting that she listen to a mass for him. The much dreaded visit of his father occurs. Sorel ceases his reproaches when Julien suggests that he will bequeath his money to his father and brothers. Julien then shares a bottle of champagne with two other prisoners and listens to the life story of one. Finally, Julien is left to his gloomy meditations.

Julien submits to confession, and provincial public opinion is thereby satisfied. Mme. de Rênal has left Verrières and, living with her aunt in Besançon, visits Julien twice a day. This bliss is interrupted by the daily visits of Mathilde. M. de Croisenois has been killed in a duel defending the honor of Mathilde. Julien angrily rejects a Jansenist's entreaties that he make a spectacular conversion, which, according to the priest, would encourage many lost souls to return to the Church. Julien must dissuade Mme. de Rênal from begging a reprieve from the king at Saint-Cloud. After the execution, Mathilde visits the cell and carries off Julien's head. Fouqué, carrying out Julien's last wishes, negotiates his burial on a high hill overlooking Verrières. Mathilde accompanies the procession and with her own hands buries Julien's head. Mme. de Rênal dies three days after the death of Julien.

Commentary

In the time of the novel, the action of Chapter 43 occurs only one hour after Mathilde had left Julien's cell in the preceding chapter. In 43, the incident of greatest importance is, of course, Mme. de Rênal's visit with Julien. Then in almost a sentence, Stendhal indicates that "three days after these visits had been taking place," M. de Rênal recalls her home. The end of the chapter elaborates another short incident, the interview of the priest, and Chapter 44 opens with the immediate reaction of Julien after the priest has left. This is typical of Stendhal's treatment of time and events. A single chapter develops one incident (already begun in what precedes), culminates it (indicating that this incident was in fact typical by multiplying its occurrence, condensing time by an allusion to its passage), and introduces a second (to be enlarged in the following chapter).

The long awaited event is the reunion of Mme. de Rênal with Julien. Stendhal tells us that Julien has never known such happiness, although the author's "pudeur" prevents him, as usual, from elaborating the ecstatic happiness that both enjoy during this supreme moment. He passes over it with: "much later, when they were able to speak." Mme. de Rênal loves Julien as a human should love only God. This is no doubt the love that Stendhal would have wanted to receive. Mme. de Rênal's sadness and admission of her disgrace prompt a "new happiness" in Julien. In Stendhal's conception of love, one constantly makes new discoveries in the object, which increases one's love for her.

We are now aware of the extent of Julien's love for Mme. de Rênal and of how instrumental it has been in his calm acceptance of the death penalty up to this point. Imagining himself bereft of her love, Julien was prepared for death. Now, a new possibility of happiness opens up before him, and he will really know the terror of the condemned man. The priest's visit serves to materialize Julien's despair, and thereafter, he sees death as horrible.

It was no doubt Stendhal's "pudeur" that prevented him from giving titles to the last four chapters in the original version of the novel. It is as if the suggestion of privacy were thus made after Julien has been condemned to death. Within one short chapter, Julien moves from the heights of bliss to the depths of despair.

Weeping about his own death, Julien will be visited, in Chapter 44, by three more "misfortunes": the visits of Mathilde and of his father, and exposure to the criminals with whom he shares a bottle of champagne.

From these he will draw food for meditation. During these meditations, the reader will witness, for the last time, Julien's solitude. There exists in this chapter the same movement as in the preceding one, but in reverse: from the depths of despair, Julien will emerge "strong and resolute, as a man who sees clearly into his own heart."

Julien finally learns about the machinations of Mathilde and Frilair. The latter, no doubt in an effort to mitigate the betrayal he has suffered personally from Valenod, has tried to shift the blame for Julien's conviction to Julien himself. Frilair sees the courtroom oration as an invitation for condemnation to death. Julien has great difficulty in concealing his despair from Mathilde. His remark concerning the prisoner's public situation vis-à-vis the world sets the tone for the chapter. Just as in life outside, Julien is forced to adopt a hypocritical air in dealing with his visitors to protect what remains of his courage.

The interlude of the prisoners is at once a moment of respite, of relief — an escape from the horror of the present moment — thereby permitting Julien to transform his self-reproach and grief into a more objective melancholy, and a pendant to the visit by his father. Both incidents are inspirational to his musings in the latter part of the chapter. The prisoner episode is reminiscent of the appearance of Géronomo at the Rênal home in Part I, which constituted a sort of poetic escape from the misfortunes of the family. Here, there is a more macabre note. Greed for money has motivated the life of this criminal, otherwise endowed with a brave heart.

Thus taken out of himself, Julien is able to recapture the necessary detachment to arrive at the re-creation of the required attitude before death. From Julien's meditations result some of the very important ingredients of beylism: the need to see man for what he is, not to be taken in, not to betray one's real nature; the danger of trading the present moment of happiness, so hard to come by, for sterile meditations about the unfathomable; in the absence of any ethical basis of society, the necessity of the creation of and adherence to a private code of morality based upon the most exigent criterium — duty toward oneself.

Five days elapsed during Chapter 44. Stendhal terminates his novel with rapidity. One would be hard put to say over what extent of time the action takes place in the final chapter. It opens as a continuation of the final scene of the preceding chapter: Fouqué awakens Julien, the latter having regained his composure and resolution. Stendhal is winding up, moving from Julien's relationship to Mme. de Rênal, to Mathilde, almost without transition.

Julien admits to Mme. de Rênal that he mistook, at the time, the real happiness he had known with her in Vergy. Mathilde is insanely jealous of Mme. de Rênal's visits, and Julien's own role toward Mathilde has now become almost paternal, just as Mme. de Rênal's love for him still has a maternal character.

Stendhal's refusal to indulge in hyperbolic description and pathos is evidenced by his very sparse treatment of the execution of Julien, which has been termed literary euthanasia. We are told that the weather was beautiful, that Julien was poetic, courageous, observant of decorum. Stendhal even makes Julien "speak" after the narration of his death, as instructions to Fouqué concerning burial are given.

Note the final utilization of the "high place" motif in the burial of Julien. The cell has been the scene of his last happiness, and the heights culminate this representation beyond death. It is fitting that Mathilde be portrayed in this macabre scene retrieving Julien's head. It permits her to play the final scene in the drama from the past which she has re-enacted in her affair with Julien. There is likewise a kind of poetic justice attained thereby — her "amour de tête" is recompensed.

One wonders at the future of Mathilde de la Mole. Stendhal has hinted, in a previous chapter, that Frilair's attempts to replace Julien had not yet been noticed by Mathilde. As for Mme. de Rênal, her death is the logical consequence of her character and conduct. She and Julien have shared a more vital identity. Mathilde and Mme. de Rênal, each reflecting aspects of Julien, are complementary.

ANALYSIS OF MAIN CHARACTERS

JULIEN SOREL

Stendhal's depiction of Julien betokens his art in conceiving beings where contradictory impulses and qualities coexist. Julien shares his gentle qualities and sentiment with Mme. de Rênal and his aggressiveness and egotism rival Mathilde's, but Julien remains, necessarily, a solitary figure whose existence is to be enjoyed by himself alone. It is the solitude, imposed from within and without, of the superior individual who requires of others their generous and voluntary self-sacrifice for his sake that emerges as the dominant trait of the Stendhalian hero, in spite of his dichotomy.

Such a hero proves himself worthy of the sacrifice made by others of the "happy few" by his observance of an ascetic personal code of honor and morality, born of and nurtured by revolt. Julien would have found lasting happiness with Mme. de Rênal, were he not a Stendhalian hero. He faces death resolutely, having arrived at the certainty that he has been faithful to his code.

From several points of view, Julien is a twentieth-century hero. He represents the individual alienated from and pitted against society, whose vileness and corruption offend his idealism and integrity as an individual. For in the last analysis, Julien chooses idealism as opposed to compromise. He is a tragic figure in that he is superior to the force that destroys him, and to the extent that he has assumed his own death, he cheats the guillotine. It is possible that Julien's amoral pose may be more acceptable than the immorality of the society that has forced him to adopt it.

MATHILDE DE LA MOLE

Mathilde is a female Julien, except that her rebellion is sterile, motivated only by a thirst for the novel, the bizarre, the unusual. In a sense, she is as much the victim of the reigning social order as is Julien, since it stifles her imagination and potential of energy. Her aggressiveness and domineering nature cause her, in effect, to play a masculine role, which explains in part the impression she gives as Julien's rival.

Her romantic temperament has been aggravated by the absence of any outlet in which to express itself. After conceiving the thought that only the death sentence could distinguish a man, she resorts to the attempt to live out this thought in real life. Her aristocratic pride is as great as Julien's fear of ridicule, and this clash proves to be an almost insurmountable obstacle to the realization of their love. Her pride and vanity thwart the expression of her romantic nature, which is somewhat the reverse of Julien's dilemma: his sensitivity constantly erupts to thwart his preconceived conduct.

Paradoxically, the character flaws that prevent them from achieving happiness are the necessary flaws of the superior being. Mathilde should not have intellectualized her passion, implies Stendhal disapprovingly, yet because of this defect, Mathilde may count herself among the "happy few." Her passion controlled by reason represents another variation of Stendhal's own impossible ideal: to love and not lose control. Like Julien, she lives in accordance with her own demanding morality. All in all, since Mathilde has fully realized her romantic dream at the end of the novel, one can visualize her as unhappy only after her last raptures have ceased, and, finding herself back in the banality of reality, she searches for a new adventure.

MADAME DE RENAL

Mme. de Rênal contrasts with Mathilde in age and in nature. The two further reflect different aspects of Julien's nature: Mme. de Rênal is spontaneous, sensitive, tenderhearted, as is Julien; Mathilde shares his pride. Mme. de Rênal awakens to a new existence when she falls in love with Julien. It is as if her previous thirty years had not existed. This sudden, overwhelming blossoming of her being explains the violence and permanence of her passion.

Her love sharpens her intelligence and endows her with momentary cunning and daring, making her again the reverse of Mathilde. At first a very moral person and somewhat naive, she sacrifices every scruple to her love for Julien. She is incapable of self-scrutiny, so instinctive a creature is she. Mme. de Rênal never achieves the amoral freedom that typifies the "happy few," although her existence on the instinctive level approximates amorality.

From her son's illness, which she sees as divine punishment, to her death following Julien's own, she is constantly tossed between passion and guilt. This fluctuation is not as obvious as it is in the case of Mathilde, but it is nonetheless basic to her nature. Mme. de Rênal can make claim to be of the "happy few," however, in that her happiness is found in love and it is doomed to failure. It is the happiness of the moment and of eternity. The maternal nature of Mme. de Rênal's love for Julien is complemented by the latter's paternal concern for Mathilde.

M. DE RÊNAL

M. de Rênal appears as the unsympathetic dupe and answers to the definition of the ridiculous character in that he contributes to his own downfall. His materialistic values are the antithesis of those of the "happy few." In Stendhal's view, the French of his time played the role of duped or of duper. M. de Rênal is, of course, in the former category. M. de Rênal is doubtless Stendhal's repudiation of his own father.

MARQUIS DE LA MOLE

Although the marquis, like the mayor, prepares his own misery in that he makes Julien his protégé, he is treated with more deference and respect by Stendhal than is the mayor. He would represent the father Stendhal would have wanted. Julien first usurps the role of son from Norbert, then that of father of Mathilde. The same pattern is visible in both families into which Julien enters: M. de Rênal cannot forsake his wife, who in turn loves Julien; M. de la Mole cannot get along without Mathilde, who is hopelessly in love with Julien. In his role of the generous father vis-à-vis the hero, M. de la Mole prefigures the same role to be played by Mosca in the *Charterhouse.*

STENDHAL'S ROMANTICISM AND REALISM

Labels always prove to be inaccurate, and at best they signal tendencies by which individuals may be grouped as more different than similar. This is particularly true of writers like Stendhal, in whom mutually exclusive tendencies coexist but achieve a kind of synthesis in the author's artistic creations. Although *The Red and the Black* appeared during the heyday of French Romanticism and the novel and Stendhal are in many ways "romantic," Stendhal seems to absent himself from his time, and while writing for the twentieth century, perpetuates the rationalism of the seventeenth century, the empiricism of the eighteenth, and announces the re-emergence of this "scientific" spirit of later nineteenth-century Realism and Naturalism.

Beylism itself, Stendhal's personal "system of happiness," shows a curious combination of romantic and realistic influences. Its ideal is romantic and, at the same time, a modification of eighteenth-century epicureanism. It assumes the existence of a superior elite, dedicated to the enjoyment of happiness, consisting of the "combined satisfaction of the intellect, imagination, and the will," as Léon Blum expresses it. Stendhal's confidence in man's ability to "systematize" happiness through experimentation announces the optimism of Comte's positivism, which, in turn, is influential in the formulation of Naturalism's scientific pretentions.

Stendhal's romantic tendencies are: the cult of the superior individual in revolt against society and its ideology; the presentation, albeit indirect, of himself idealized in his protagonists, indicating a basic subjectivity; the portrayal of sensitive, passionate souls on the quest for happiness — happiness, again, such as the author himself conceives.

These romantic traits are constantly subdued, however, by traits that make Stendhal a realist or classicist. He is attached to reality, specifically to contemporary reality, which he would render with scrupulous honesty and exactness. Julien is what Stendhal would want to be, but at the same time Julien is Antoine Berthet, and the society he encounters is that which confronts Berthet. Although many of Stendhal's characters are "beylistes," they are formed by their environment, as registered by their sensorial impressions, and this psychological process is portrayed as such by the author. In true classical tradition, Stendhal's study is of man's inner life, fraught with conflict, although Stendhal has no didactic aims, except perhaps as manifested in his desire to reach the "happy few."

Stendhal's own hypercritical attitude toward himself dictates his treatment of his characters, whom he "puts to the test," throwing them into predicaments where their worth may be measured. Stendhal's resulting detachment from his creatures creates the air of an ironic objectivity.

He forged his style in direct reaction to the lyrical, hyperbolic, flowery style of Romanticism. Constantly checking his own extreme sensibility, Stendhal trusted only the authenticity of spontaneity and created a style, which in its directness, approximates the immediacy of the spoken language. The Stendhalian sentence is clipped, dry, terse, and has an irregular cadence in its rapidity. Although it is as far from Flaubert's laboriously wrought prose as from the hyperbole of the romantics, Stendhal's style is realistic in a broader sense of the term, in that it communicates a direct impression of life being lived at the present moment.

REVIEW QUESTIONS AND THEME TOPICS

1. Justify, if possible, the political episodes as not being extraneous to Julien's individual drama.

2. Exemplify Stendhal's "tender irony" toward his "happy few."

3. Does the attempted murder of Mme. de Rênal by Julien contradict his character or is it consistent with the hero's nature?

4. What could be an explanation for Stendhal's use of epigraphs preceding every chapter?

5. Is it the realism or romanticism of the novel that appeals to the contemporary audience of Stendhal?

6. Determine to what extent Julien is an aggressive protagonist, actively responsible for his successes and failures.

7. Compare the two parts of the novel from the point of view of structure and recurrence of motifs.

8. How does Stendhal maintain the reader's sympathy for his hero?

9. Which character — Mme. de Rênal or Mathilde de la Mole — do you find more convincing?

10. How does Julien's affair with Mathilde reflect the political conflict exposed in the novel?

11. Does Julien commit suicide?

12. In what ways is Stendhal's improvisational technique apparent in the novel?

13. To what extent are the characters the victims of self-delusion?

14. Define Stendhal's method of psychological analysis.

SELECTED BIBLIOGRAPHY

In English

Adams, Robert M. *Stendhal: Notes on a Novelist.* New York: The Noonday Press, 1959. An amusing, highly original work which confronts influences that Stendhal underwent, with their reflection in his novels. The author gives the impression of imitating Stendhal's improvisational technique.

Brombert, Victor. *Stendhal, a Collection of Critical Essays.* Englewood Cliffs, N.J.: Prentice-Hall, Inc., 1962. A very useful collection of essays with an equally informative preface by the editor. Six of the essays treat various aspects of different novels; five are devoted to the novelist, alluding directly to his philosophy or style. The essays are excerpted from entire works.

Dutourd, Jean. *The Man of Sensibility,* (translated from the French by Robin Chancellor). New York: Simon & Schuster, 1961. An original and unique approach to Stendhal that embraces both Stendhal and his good friend Mérimée, by using the latter's essay on Stendhal ("H.B.," 1850) as a point of departure for each chapter of his own criticism. Dutourd emphasizes Stendhal's modernity.

Green, F. C. *Stendhal.* Cambridge: Cambridge University Press, 1939. A solid interpretation of the works of a very contradictory author.

Recommended for the individual who is baffled by the enigmatic Stendhal and is looking for some clear interpretations.

Levin, Harry. *The Gates of Horn.* New York: Oxford University Press, 1963. (The chapter herein contained was originally published as *Toward Stendhal;* New Directions, 1945.) A very provocative study of Stendhal's works as an expression and representation of his time. Levin sees Stendhal as a reformed idealist, the first in the current of bourgeois literature that is Realism.

In French

Bardèche, Maurice. *Stendhal romancier.* Paris: La Table ronde, 1947. Bardèche treats Beyle principally as a novelist. He probes the circumstances and sources of composition and offers helpful interpretations of the novels.

Caraccio. Armand. *Stendhal, L'Homme et L'Oeuvre* (Connaissance des Lettres series). Paris: Boivin et Cie., 1951. The first part is devoted to the author's life, the second to his works. Caraccio's concluding chapter reviews briefly Stendhal criticism. Although the work is not exhaustive, it is reliable and entertaining.

Marill-Albérès, Francine. *Stendhal* (Classiques du XIXe Siècle series). Paris: Editions Universitaires, 1959. A short work devoted to Stendhal's works and offering a poeticized interpretation of the "Stendhalian universe."

Martineau, Henri. *L'Oeuvre de Stendhal.* Paris: Le Divan, 1945. The great French Stendhal scholar presents an authoritative, basic study of the works and thought of Stendhal. He traces the author's thought by chronologically following his works. It is primarily a study in literary history rather than in interpretation.

————. *Le Coeur de Stendhal.* 2 vols. Paris; A. Michel, 1952, 1953. Rated as the best biography of Stendhal.

Prévost, Jean. *La Création chez Stendhal.* Paris: Mercure de France, 1951. As the title indicates, the work is devoted to an investigation of the creative process of the author as deduced from his works, and to a very imaginative analysis of style: character presentation and utilization, narrative techniques, and stylistic devices.

NOTES

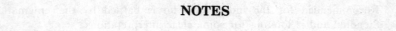

NOTES

NOTES

NOTES

NOTES

NOTES

NOTES